THE PSYCHOLOGY OF ENLIGHTENMENT:
MEDITATIONS ON THE SEVEN ENERGY CENTERS

THE PSYCHOLOGY OF ENLIGHTENMENT:

MEDITATIONS ON THE SEVEN ENERGY CENTERS

BY

Gurudev Shree Chitrabhanu

Edited by Lyssa Miller

DODD, MEAD & COMPANY
NEW YORK

1   2   3   4   5   6   7   8   9   10

Library of Congress Cataloging in Publication Data

_____

The psychology of enlightenment.

    1.   Religious life (Jainism) —Meditations.
I.   Miller, Lyssa.   II.   Title.
BL1378.6.C46   294.4′4′3   79-795
ISBN 0-396-07676-9

For information
regarding current program,
please contact

 **Meditation
International
Center**
120 East 86th Street,
New York City
212-722-7474.

Contents

Contents

[v]

About the Author

One of the spiritual leaders of India's four million Jains, Gurudev Shree Chitrabhanu is the first Jain master to come to the United States.

He arrived in America in 1971, when he accepted the invitation of the Temple of Understanding to address the Spiritual Summit Conference held at Harvard Divinity School. Since then, he has lectured throughout the East Coast at universities and preparatory schools and, in 1974, was the keynote speaker at the Quaker Conference on World Peace at Cornell University. He has worked closely with the World Fellowship of Religions, the United Nations, and other globally minded organizations. Presently, Gurudev Chitrabhanu is spiritual adviser to the Jain Meditation International Center in New York and to other meditation centers in the United States, Brazil, and India.

Gurudev's philosophy is that of reverence for all life. His lectures aim at kindling awareness of the Self within each of us. He teaches meditation as an integral part of daily living, not as an escape from reality, but as a means to a richer, more satisfying life.

A teacher of universal scope, Gurudev Chitrabhanu has said, "I do not want to teach people their duties or any doctrine of religion. I want to arouse them from their complacencies, to stir their hearts, to vivify their imagination, to bring them from their little selves to the Higher, of which they are capable."

THE IMMORTAL SONG

May the sacred stream of amity flow forever in my heart,
May the universe prosper, such is my cherished desire;
May my heart sing with ecstasy at the sight of the virtuous,
And may my life be an offering at their feet.
May the heart bleed at the sight of the wretched, the cruel, and the
    poor,
And may tears of compassion flow from my eyes;
May I always be there to show the path to the pathless wanderers
    of life,
Yet if they should not hearken to me, may I bide patiently,
May the spirit of goodwill enter into all our hearts,
May we all sing together the immortal song of brotherhood,
The immortal song of sisterhood,
The immortal song of brotherhood. . . .

—CHITRABHANU

How to Use This Book

The Psychology of Enlightenment: Meditations on the Seven Energy Centers is a meditation handbook. Its purpose is to instruct students of meditation in a technique for unfolding and experiencing their inner energy, as developed by the ancient meditative traditions in India. According to this teaching, there are seven centers of energy within the body, corresponding to seven levels of consciousness or awareness. Through these centers, we experience different aspects of our inner life-force. The flow of energy at each of these points may be partially obstructed by our accumulated fears, our unchecked drives, and our wrong perception. Through meditation, we are able to recognize and remove these hindrances and restore the flow of our creative life-energy.

This book is based on a series of lectures given by Gurudev Shree Chitrabhanu. Each of the first seven chapters deals with a specific energy center and suggests a method of meditation for that particular aspect of energy. The eighth chapter applies the psychology of the seven centers to gain-

[xi]

ing and maintaining your health, and the ninth chapter combines the centers in a single meditation.

It is suggested that the student take one energy center per week for his or her meditation practice. The student will find that the technique in this book has two aspects: visualization and the use of a mantra. A specific mantra and visual symbol are suggested for each energy center. Occasionally the student may have a choice of visual symbols. In these cases, he or she is free to experiment and to choose the symbol that feels most natural.

The use of a mantra is an integral part of these meditations. It will be helpful to think of each mantra as a key which opens a particular door, unlocks a particular aspect of energy. Some students, however, may prefer to use only one mantra. For these students, there is the master key, *sohum*. This mantra is capable of opening all doors.

Focusing on one center per week, students may use this mantra in their meditation. *Sohum,* which means "I am That," is not a substitute for the suggested mantras, but an alternative to them. Through *sohum* ("I am That"), we gradually perceive what "That" is: The Self, the Real, the Permanent, our True Nature, Love. As we come to know our real nature, we begin to enjoy the sense of an enduring security at the first center. At the second energy center, our feelings of inadequacy give way to a new surge of creative vitality. Then we experience the power of natural expression and communion with those around us through the third center.

Sohum, the mantra for the fourth center at the heart, ignites in us the spark of love for all our fellow beings. As our loving embrace gradually encompasses the whole universe, we discover, at the fifth center, that this universe is our bountiful friend. The process of focusing our attention on the meaning of *sohum* points out to us the difference between our enduring soul and our temporary material body. At the sixth center, we learn to identify with "That," our consciousness, rather than with the body. Then we begin to disengage ourselves from the constant, restless game of life so that we can observe the quality of our playing. We can perceive the world as it really is; we can distinguish between appearance and reality. Ultimately, at the seventh center, there is no longer any separation between the "I" and the "That" of *sohum*. We realize simply that we are, that there is only pure awareness.

As a link between our present awareness and our true, pure nature, *sohum* is a powerful tool for our meditations on these centers. Although each of these centers has its particular mantra, many masters in the past have reached enlightenment using this key mantra. Students of meditation can choose either approach in their practice on the seven centers. Both are valid and both will lead to the ultimate goal: the experience of Self.

A Guide to Pronouncing Sanskrit Words

The following is a partial explanation of the pronunciation of Sanskrit words to aid you in using the names and mantras in this book.

Vowels: Each vowel in Sanskrit is divided into long and short. The long vowels are indicated by a straight line above the letter, as in *ā, ī, ū*. Sanskrit words are pronounced evenly without accenting a particular syllable. Vowel sounds are similar to those in Italian.

vowel	*English equivalent*
a	*u*p or s*u*m
ā	f*a*ther
i	d*i*m
ī	d*ee*m
u	t*oo*th
ū	m*oo*n

r—is considered a semi-vowel. It is spoken
   slightly rolled, as in the Italian *signore*.

NOTE: In this text, the mantra *sohum* has been written phonetically to make it less confusing to the reader. The vowel in *hum* is actually a short *a* which sounds like *u* in the English *sum*.

Consonants: The *h* following a consonant is audibly and separately pronounced. For example, the name of the first center, *mulādhāra*, is pronounced *mu·lā·d·hā·ra*.

The same rule applies for the combination *th*. In other words, *th* in Sanskrit is not pronounced as in the English *think*. For example, the name of the second center is *swādhisthāna*, pronounced *swād·his·t·hā·na*.

The hard *g* sound, as in *good*, is sometimes written as *j*, as in the name for the sixth center, *ājnā*, which is pronounced *āgnā*.

Author's Foreword

It will be helpful for us to think of this human body as a musical instrument having seven notes, seven different rates of vibration. Each note has its own unique place in music. If we are confined to playing only one note, the sound we produce will be monotonous. So, we are here to learn how to create the harmonious, melodious music of life. Through the guidance of a master, we can learn to play our own music with this instrument. We can learn to be independent music makers who will be a source of inspiration to others. If our instrument is to create beautiful, soothing music, the life-force must be able to move freely from note to note, from the base of the spine to the crown of the head.

In ancient times, these seven centers were taught only to advanced students of meditation—those who had successfully completed a series of tests, those who had been initiated into an inner circle, or those who a master knew to be ready for the teaching. Only those students who have fully absorbed the lessons of the beginning stages of meditation can truly appreciate the value of these seven centers.*

Today we naïvely believe we can put our money down and learn a little something about meditation. It is true that we may come away with a few new ideas about how to relax and how to relieve some of our tension; but will money unfold our consciousness or give us a deep experience of the meaning and purpose of life? No, of course not. That takes a lifetime of patient practice. We are too easily satisfied with too little. Mankind does not realize the magnitude of his inner energy, nor does he understand that there is a fathomless ocean of knowledge lying within.

Many of us have not yet discovered that inner Self which is real and permanent. This Self, this soul, is invisible. What, then, do we see when we visualize in our meditation? We see that energy which is a manifestation of the invisible soul. Have you ever felt a cool breeze brush against your arm? You know that you are feeling the coolness of air although you cannot see it. Similarly, in meditation, through both your intuitive feeling and your inner vision, you will begin to experience that of which you have been unaware: the invisible soul.

Someone once said that in order to find joy in living, there must be something worth dying for. What did he mean by this? Here, dying means not the death of the physical body but the giving up or losing of a lesser thing in order to awaken to something greater. In other words, one must relinquish something of secondary importance before

* For a guide to beginning meditation, see: Chitrabhanu, *Realize What You Are: The Fundamentals of Jain Meditation*

one can appreciate and enjoy something of primary importance.

Consider a cube of sugar, for example. In order for the sugar to impart its true sweetness, to fulfill its real potential, it must first lose its temporary rigid form. It must dissolve. Therefore, when we place a cube of sugar in a cup of warm milk, it naturally gives up its shape, releasing its sweet flavor. If, however, that sugar were able to identify with being a cube and cling to its cube-nature, it would not dissolve and would not realize its hidden sweetness, its true sugar-nature.

We are not so different from this sugar cube. We must first give up our small ego—our self-imposed limitations, our fears, our feelings of inadequacy and impotence, and our identification with temporary gains and losses. When we have dissolved these, all that will remain is the sweet essence of our Real Self. Only then will our lives be fully illumined by our invisible soul. In this sense, losing is our gain, our real and permanent gain.

It is easy to talk about meditation on the seven centers, but difficult to practice. It takes years. The results of meditation depend not upon my descriptions, but upon your sincere and consistent practice.

—CHITRABHANU
New York, 1978

CHAPTER I

Mulādhāra—
The Seat of Security

The world is divided into three kinds of people. First and most common are those whose life-energy is spent killing time. For them, life has no meaning other than eating and drinking and grasping for enjoyment, which always eludes them. They are like human machines, seeing and suspecting nothing beyond the limited scope of their own machine. Killing time, they kill their own energy and drain the energy of those around them. Time merely passes for them.

The second kind are those who want to do something with their time and energy, but don't know what to do. They are confused in their pursuit of various techniques and books and in their choice of paths. Lacking direction, they do not grow. Though they may read a great deal, their reading does not bring inner nourishment. These people lack the sense of discrimination, so their search leads nowhere.

The third kind are those individuals who turn to their

[1]

own inner experience for counsel. They have embarked on a real journey to the inner Self wherein lie all life's answers. They know that if the answer is not found within, it surely cannot be found anywhere outside.

When we consider the example of those dynamic individuals like Einstein, for instance, who have brought some gift of themselves to mankind and changed the face of the world, we must realize that we, too, possess a hidden treasure within: the gift of infinite potential. We have the same capacity for unfolding our latent talents and energy as they do. What is possible for one human being is possible for each of us.

Then what can we do to manifest our infinite potential? We begin by believing that this capacity exists in us. Now we believe in God, in a guru, in religion, in someone or something other than ourselves. It is easy to believe in others because there is no work involved. It is very easy to put our faith in an outside God because He is invisible. He does not interfere with our plans and desires. We can participate with Him in our imagination and mold our idea of Him according to our need. It is far more difficult to love another person, or even ourselves, because there is a tangible relationship. So, the first step is to stop relying on something outside ourselves. We must believe, instead, in our own infinite reservoirs of strength and vitality.

What kind of person do we want to be? The decision is up to us. Shall we simply pass the time allotted to us in a meaningless round of temporary pleasures? Shall we scatter our precious life-energy in a dozen directions that lead nowhere? Or shall we choose, instead, to go in the direction of growth, to gain wisdom and insight from our experience of life, and to discover and unfold our unique qualities?

To reach our goal, whatever it may be, it is necessary that we remain single-minded in our effort, although the mind will no doubt tempt us to go in a hundred different directions. My teacher once asked us, "If you were looking for water, would you drill fifty holes of one-foot depth or one hole that was fifty feet deep?" In either case, the effort is the same, but the results are different. We can choose to dissipate our energy in a variety of fruitless, incomplete attempts to find water, or we can concentrate our attention, time, and muscle-power on digging in the direction of water until we tap it. The choice is ours.

To move in the direction of growth requires the persistent study of one's own Self. How do you study the Self? Begin simply by asking, "What is man? Who am I?" Stop identifying with those things which are given to you by society, like your name and title, or other concepts, such as success or failure, beauty or ugliness. These are, after all, only relative values. For instance, what appears attractive in one culture may be considered ugly in another. You know there are people in parts of Africa who wear ornaments which stretch their earlobes or pierce their noses. If these people were to come to the West, they would look strange; but for them, long ears or a pierced nose are signs of beauty.

Concepts are not absolutes; they are all your own projections. They keep you revolving around the periphery of life and prevent you from coming in touch with the core of your being. Go beyond them and ask, "Who am I really?

Who is moving? Who is eating? Who is meeting? Who is doing all these things?" The fundamental question is this: "Who am I?"

At first we may not get an immediate answer to "Who am I?" because we are in the habit of imitating others. We dress according to the fashion out of fear of not being accepted. We laugh when other people laugh. Most of us don't feel secure unless we conform to the people around us, so we seldom act according to our true nature. We act, instead, as someone else might act. The result is conflict. Subconsciously, we recognize this; but consciously, we forget it. We forget because we have so many distractions, so many appointments and activities, so many fantasies and expectations.

When we seriously ask, "Who am I?" we become aware of the conflict between what we have been taught to think we ought to be and what we really are. It begins to dawn on us that we have not been living correctly. That is when we turn inward to discover the exact nature of our body, our mind, and finally, the inside dweller which is our true Self.

The seven levels of consciousness or energy centers on which we will meditate are nothing but points of awareness from which we can begin to discern our true nature. In our journey to the seventh and highest point, we must beware of haste and spiritual greed. Our eagerness may tempt us to grab impatiently for our goal, but our success depends instead upon gradually letting go. What is it, after all, that we imagine we are grabbing for? It can only be our fantasy—some preconceived idea. What do we hope to gain by our hurry? Overnight enlightenment is a false promise which leads inevitably to disappointment and feelings of worthlessness. The momentary height which is reached in haste has no substance; it will burst like a bubble. Only that growth which is a gradual unfolding can endure.

This mind of ours is impatient. It demands instant answers and immediate results. There is a story of a rich man who wanted to send his son to the university, but he wanted him to graduate in just two years so that he could go into the family business. The old man offered to pay double if his son could be graduated early. The dean said to the father, "Well, I can graduate your son early, but first tell me one thing. You must know what you are settling for. You must decide if you want parsley or an oak tree. It does not take long to grow parsley, but an oak tree takes years of careful nurturing and growth before it matures. Tell me, is it a little sprig of parsley you want or a mighty oak?"

If we are searching for the mighty oak, for the wellspring of our creative potential, for the real answer to "Who am I?" then we must give up the idea of instant enlightenment and be willing to work consistently and sincerely.

The first step is to consider the body. It is composed of four essential elements which ancient traditions called earth, water, fire, and air. You will not find any organism in which these four elements are missing. Now, each of these elements has its corresponding element in the universe. The earth element within the body, for instance, corresponds or vibrates with the earth element throughout the universe.

What composes the body or microcosm also constitutes

the universe or macrocosm. There is a deep innate relationship between the microcosm and macrocosm, and we are capable of building a deep harmony between the two. Those who know how to build harmony are going to remain in balance, and those who are in balance enjoy health of mind and body. Sickness is nothing but imbalance, so where there is harmony, there is health.

Ancient cultures understood this relationship between mankind and the universal elements. They recognized the universal earth element as the soil, the ground, the foundation on which we sit and walk and grow. When they searched for man's own corresponding foundation, they found a point at the bottom vertebrae where we sit. This point is referred to in Sanskrit as *mulādhāra. Mula* means "root," and *ādhāra* means "support." It is the root by which the structure is supported. In other words, the whole structure is balancing itself on that support which is the lowest point of our spinal column.

This is the first point of awareness from which we can transform our feelings of insecurity into a solid foundation of self-reliance. Here we come into contact with the earth element and the earthly desire to acquire, to hoard. In the old days it was common for people to bury gold coins for safekeeping. Times haven't changed! Recently, a gentleman casually mentioned to me, "I trust gold so much that whenever I save some money, I buy guineas and hide them away somewhere!"

What is this desire to hide, to bury, to hold onto things? What makes a person think that way? Insecurity. Man is insecure even when he has abundance. People fear that

[6]

someday they may lose their possessions. They do not realize that eventually possessions must go because it is their nature to go. No matter how carefully you collect and preserve your wealth, it will one day leave you. If it does not first leave you, you know that you yourself will inevitably depart. One of the two things will happen.

In effect, we are investing our energy in the fear of future want. Our habit of comparing what we have now with what others possess produces this sense of insecurity, which denies us the capacity to enjoy what we have already. It is a kind of addiction which brings anxiety and drives us to amass more than we need. With this mental addiction to achieving a sense of security through possession of more and more things, man no longer remembers what he originally meant by "more." The word "more" is all right, but how much more? He does not know. Wealth and security are always relative terms, and they seem always just out of reach.

When we judge ourselves by other people's standards, we foster feelings of insecurity. Somehow, we haven't learned that we will never find peace as long as we worry about what others may think of us. Why bother about them? Can we not let go and give them liberty to think what they will of us? If they become happy thinking ill of us, let them be happy.

When you learn the art of living, you will know that as long as you do not think negatively of yourself, negativity is not going to affect you. The law is this: Negativity hurts only those who think negatively of themselves. We are hurt only by our own low opinion of ourselves. The whole problem of insecurity and feelings of inadequacy actually comes from within, and the only way to heal this inner wound is not to think ill of ourselves even for a moment. No guilt. This is the secret found in ancient teachings which state, "You are nothing but God within. You are covering this divinity with your human form. You are Brahman. You are Paramātmā, the Supreme Soul." Your positivity can become a castle around you which will protect you from the arrow of negativity.

If you accept that there is divinity in you, your divine nature will gradually become apparent. It is not a question of bragging to people that you are God. Bragging is egotistical, but experiencing the truth is altogether different. When you accept that inner divinity, you understand that the immortal Soul is living in this body temporarily. Your divinity is incognito. It may be difficult to accept this idea at first because we have been hampered by guilt for such a long time. We have been taught to think of ourselves as worthless sinners. However, if we now acknowledge the possibility of this beautiful dweller residing in all of us, our whole approach to the world will change. We will be able to say, "Let the world say what it will. I know what I am and who I am. If the world wants to agree with me, let it. If it does not want to agree with me, let it. I know myself. I do not live by the words and opinions of others. I know who I am. I am God incognito." Eventually, people will sense that you know your true nature. When you acknowledge and respect your real Self, the world, in turn, will acknowledge and respect you.

Therefore, friends, our first step is to give up this insecu-

[8]

rity which spoils our ability to enjoy what we have right now. We must remember that insecurity is not our inborn nature. It is a mental creation and an addiction born of our cultural programming. We can retrain our minds by focusing our attention on the seven energy centers. As we do, we will find life becoming so smooth that we will enjoy whatever life brings. Each moment of life will turn into joy. This is important because the years which we have will not come back. These are the beautiful years, so why should we waste these precious moments worrying about the future and upset about what other people may be thinking of us? We can choose, instead, to start now unfolding the infinite potential within. For this we need self-confidence and emotional independence. We can begin to develop these qualities by meditating on the point of awareness at the base of the spine, the earth center, our foundation.

Take time for your daily meditation either first thing in the morning or at evening after your day's work. In the morning, you are fresh; your body is rested and full of energy, and your mind is not yet engaged in the activities of the day. In the evening, you can put aside the day's problems and plans for the future and focus on the present moment. As you experiment with your meditation, you will discover which is the best time of day for you.

Now relax and say to yourself, "I shall come in touch with this earth element. I know this whole universe belongs to me and I am a part of the universe. Acquiring things will not bring me real security. I know that I am always secure when I feel my oneness with the universe. I am God incognito. What does it matter if the people I meet don't recognize the divinity in me? It is better that I am able to move incognito in the world."

Sit with a straight spine in a chair or on the floor, whichever is more comfortable for you. When the spine is erect, you can easily take your awareness to the base of the spinal column. Closing your eyes, visualize yourself sitting on a lovely square seat in the center of a beautiful yellow lotus blossom. The symbol of the square is important because its four corners link us to the cosmos in four directions: north, south, east, and west.

An alternative symbol for this center is a cross within a wheel or circle. (The Sanskrit word for this wheel is *chakra.* The energy centers are often referred to as the seven *chakras.*) Like the corners of the square, the four lines of the cross also connect us to the four directions.

If we focus our attention on this cross, we will see that one line is horizontal; the other, vertical. The horizontal line by itself resembles the minus sign in mathematics. Adding the vertical to the horizontal transforms the minus to plus. We, too, can turn the minus aspects of our lives to plus. We can move from feelings of emptiness (the minus) to feelings of worthiness and meaning (the plus). We may see the world as horizontal in relation to the divine, which is symbolically vertical. The earthly things we have accumulated on the horizontal plane cannot accompany us at death. In that respect, they are insignificant in the face of the vertical divine. Meditation lifts our energy along this vertical line.

The color yellow is significant because it symbolically connects us to that Higher Self which is genuine and lasting in us. Yellow is the color of gold, which, as we all know, is a precious metal mined from the earth. Gold can withstand even the test of fire, for when the dross has burned away, only the genuine element remains. In the same way, those who meditate on the earth center are no longer driven by cravings for outer security because they are in touch with something within themselves which is real and immortal. They live without fear because they know that this inner Self cannot be destroyed under any circumstances.

So, imagine yourself connected in all directions with the macrocosm, resting peacefully in the heart of the lotus. Now silently recite the mantra *shivam shānti,* which means "benediction and peace." Just be. Be one with benediction and peace. Here there is no fear or anxiety or insecurity. Just be and let go. Allow all the labels and projections to disappear. Watch any pictures or memories that pass before your mental eye. Ask yourself why you allow negative feelings and unpleasant situations to intrude on your inner peace. What are your mental addictions? What is your emotional programming? It is your programming which makes you feel secure or insecure, not the objects you seek or the events you play out. After all, those who have a different set of built-in emotional responses do not share your reactions to these same objects and circumstances. These mental and emotional addictions will gradually fall away from you under your scrutiny, and you will enjoy a new sense of calm.

As your meditation continues, feel yourself to be nothing but flowing energy. Feel only energy. Know that you are communicating with the earth element at this center of security at the bottom of the spine. This beautiful lotus gives you a sense of peace and a pleasant fragrance within a frame of beauty. Be aware that your body, too, is a frame of beauty in the center of which lives the inside dweller which is Pure Consciousness.

If you are truly in tune with this meditation, you will eventually notice that your sense of smell has become very keen and pleasant, and that you can smell things even from a distance. Each of your five senses has its corresponding energy center within the body. As you meditate on each center, your sight, hearing, taste, touch, and smell all become very sharp.

Perhaps you now rely on pills and medicines to maintain your health; but, as your mood becomes balanced through meditation, you will become healthy naturally. What you have been getting in a gross form through medication, you will get in a subtle form from the universal energy. This is a whole new concept: You can draw energy directly from the universe when you are in tune with yourself because you and the universe are one.

Meditating on the first center of awareness will help us to be relaxed, calm, and in tune with the macrocosm. Our communication with the world will become very smooth and gentle and free from friction. This is the whole art of living. Start now. Bring the energy of benediction and peace into your daily life and open yourself to the experience of profound well-being.

CHAPTER II

Swādhisthāna—Source
of Creative Potential

Human life is a cohesive whole comprised of two polarities—physical, creative, sexual energy on the one hand, and divine spiritual energy on the other. Just as east and west, north and south, are inevitable complementary points of direction, so are these two energies equal counterparts to one another. Both are essential to our life and growth. When we comprehend the intrinsic relationship between these powerful energies, we will come to understand human life more fully.

Therefore, the second point on which we will meditate is the place of our physical origin, the second center, located at the pelvis area, from which flows all our creative and productive energy. First, we ask ourselves, "What is the purpose of this creative energy? Is it for our temporary satisfaction or is it something to be suppressed? What is its nature?"

As we meditate deeply on this question, we will begin to recognize intimations of our own beginning and the poten-

[13]

tial for a loving and mutually fulfilling relationship with another human being. We will then naturally discard the idea of sin and guilt. After all, one cannot reach the end of a journey without first experiencing its beginning. So, in a sense, the beginning is included in the end. How, then, can we enjoy a blameless end if we have devalued our beginning?

I have seen people whose glimpse of spiritual awareness was limited by a lingering sense of guilt about their sexuality. They could not let go of the idea that sex is ugly. Such people cannot be truly pious as long as they continue to degrade the process of their own birth by calling it sinful. Too often, these same people mistakenly believe they are free from sexual desire while harboring a hidden, unrecognized longing. The result is anxiety and tension. Obsessed with a subtle curiosity, their minds are continually tempted by every form of sensual suggestion.

We tend to forget that we develop from one stage of life and growth to another and that each stage, from beginning to end, has its proper function. For example, it does not occur to a grown man to criticize himself for having built castles in the sand when he was a little boy. He recognizes that by building sand castles as a child, he learned how to give form to his ideas as an adult. Such childhood experiences bestow a foundation of wisdom to all subsequent stages of our life. We should approach the second center of meditation with this idea in mind and appreciate it as the center of our origin, the place of our creation.

As we learn to value this center of creativity and begin to understand it from a new perspective, we will realize that we should not squander this precious energy on temporary enjoyment or on the momentary release of tension. To spend our energy wastefully is the inevitable consequence of failing to see its importance in maintaining the body and in making our life complete. We are in the habit of dividing the body into separate, unrelated parts. By assigning different meaning and worth to each part, we have created an unnatural tension between inner feeling and outer reality. Too often, we allow ourselves to be hypocritical, outwardly professing one set of values while inwardly failing to acknowledge our hidden desire and curiosity. Why, for instance, do we feel more comfortable seeing a naked child than we do seeing a nude adult? Why? Because at that moment, we are focused, not on the totality of the adult standing before us, but only on a single aspect which we have mentally separated from the rest. Now, instead, we begin to appreciate the human being as a whole, and we recognize that each part of the body is significant only in relation to the others. The eyes, mouth, ears, hands, inner organs, and so forth, all cooperate for the benefit of the entire organism. When we comprehend the whole, we no longer segregate and devalue the parts.

So it follows that we do ourselves and our partners a grave injustice when we focus on just the sexual aspect of our relationship, spending this energy merely for temporary satisfaction. We not only deny ourselves the joy of being in tune with the whole of life, but also exclude our partner from participating in our understanding. One thing is true: Any relationship built on lust and sex alone is not going to last long. That relationship is no different from a person going to a restaurant. When the hunger is satisfied and the thirst is quenched, there is no further need to continue eating and drinking. Naturally, you leave the restaurant. Those who live on the level of temporary sexual gratification have not understood the nature of love.

Real love is peaceful; it encourages us to enjoy simply being and communing with one another, sharing our thoughts and understanding of life. Real love does not end. Excitement continually ends. When you reach the end of your excitement, where do you go? You go back where you started. With love, however, there is no such dead end. It is always moving toward eternity. Love is eternally creative because it has no finish.

When this second energy center is truly flowing and creative, there is love. Then you live comfortably with your partner, free from the need to concoct some artificial excitement or mentally rehearse what you are going to do, how you are going to meet, or what you should say. After all, where is the reality when you merely copy your mental rehearsal? Such mental games prevent you from experiencing real gentleness and genuine communication.

It may be helpful for you to know that the teaching about this energy center originated in the East several thousand years ago in an atmosphere where the relationship between man and woman was considered very sacred. Their bodies were thought of not as houses of potential sin and guilt, but as sanctified love temples in which two souls came together in a holy communion. The warmth of their love protected them as they remained together throughout eternity. They did not imagine their relationship as ending in death, but saw it instead as a perpetual thread of meeting and love from lifetime to lifetime. Often, at their first meeting, a young couple would sense that they were com-

ing together now because they had known one another before somewhere, and that they would meet yet again in the
future.

The teaching evolved out of a cultural perspective very
different from today's world, where the pursuit of immediate and temporary gratification too often leads to frustrated
expectations and hatred between partners. The teaching
acknowledges the presence in all of us of a meaningful,
creative power which unites two people even when they are
in a state of meditation. There is no hurry, no show, no
anxiety about what you should do or how you should do it.
You are tranquil.

You will be interested to know that there are many ex-
amples of couples who married young and, after creating
children, remained together for years without the need for
sexual gratification. They enjoyed each other's company
and were not at all unhappy because they had not been
brainwashed into believing that the whole meaning of marriage is sex. Those who enter married life preoccupied
with sexual gratification start hating and blaming one another when they don't get fulfillment. The whole relationship becomes very ugly. Ultimately, the marriage ends in
depression and divorce.

However, if two people approach their marriage with
the idea that they are meeting to build a life together and
complement one another, then sex comes naturally and
spontaneously. It is not a prerehearsed event. Sex neither
joins the two lives together when it is present, nor breaks
them apart when it is absent, because the two lives are connected by a larger feeling of total creativity.

No matter what creative endeavor you attempt, you may

eventually feel the need for someone with whom to share it—someone who will bring to the experience an energy of a different, but compatible, nature. Male and female are like two complementary electrical currents. Each has its unique, inborn quality and each serves the cause of human evolution, the cause of perfection. We must endeavor to discover and develop the real feminine and masculine natures without distorting them with concepts borrowed from the outside world.

Many teachers would not have you meditate on the second center because they feel that generally people mistakenly believe that the sole purpose of this energy is to enhance sexual pleasure. If that were true, then meditating on this center would only stimulate your appetite for sex. I am teaching you about the second center because I believe that ultimately you must go beyond such a limited view of this powerful force in order to embrace the creative wholeness of life.

When you meditate on the second center, you are refining your energy. Just as crude oil must go through several stages of purification before it becomes a substance fine enough to fuel a jet engine, so we also must remove any dross, any gross elements, before our energy can take us upward. Our energy must be refined if we are to enjoy a life free of turmoil—a life of bliss, peace, and clarity of perception.

The universal law is that we are free to be whatever we like. Why, then, are a few people dynamic, positive, and balanced while the majority seem to be hampered by feelings of inadequacy? Why do we so often see our problems

magnified? No one stops us from being happy, creative, secure, and enlightened; yet we are afraid to leave behind
the familiar habits of negative thinking. Why? Why don't
we realize that every problem has a solution just as every
lock has a right key? Our difficulty is that our daily haste
and confusion prevent us from discovering the key that is
needed. If we have refined our energy, however, it will
guide us in the right time to the right place.

This purified energy is not indecisive and confused, nor
is it scattered in all directions. It has the power to dissolve
all feelings of impotence and free us from the conceptual
limitations that block our creativity in any area of our life.
If we have believed that others are luckier than we are—
that they are more gifted and showered by grace—then
now is the time for us to realize that all human beings are
touched by the same divine element. When the mental
concept of limitation is lifted, then the door of our creativity is opened. Our inner store of energy is made available to us when we make a positive decision and take a step
in a definite direction. We will discover that life offers us
whatever we believe it will offer us. So when we meditate,
let us give up our preconceived images and expectations—
and all the tension and unhappiness that spring from them
—so that we may become natural and our minds may· become very pure and clear. Then we will enjoy our inherent
creativity.

The second center, located at the pelvis area, is called
swādhisthāna in Sanskrit, which means "the place of our
origin." *Swa* means "your own" and *adhisthāna* means

"dwelling, residence, or origin." As the element of the first center is earth, representing our foundation, so the element of the second is water, symbolizing our creative energy. Be aware of this element within the blood flowing through your veins and within all the cells of your body. Generally, meditation on this center will increase the sense of taste because of the presence of water in the saliva. As you master each element making up the body, you will be able to control and guide your energy wherever it is needed and effect a healing change.

The visual symbol of this center is a crescent. Just as you know that the crescent moon will develop into a beautiful full moon—a circle of perfection—so you are reminded by this symbol that you also are gradually moving toward your perfection. The color of this crescent is silver, which is bright and shining. In the same way, every human being can be illumined by the force of the inner flow of his own creative energy. If, as you visualize, you link the image to your feeling of energy, your visualization will not be an artificial projection. It will be, instead, a significant experience for you.

So, as you close your eyes, imagine yourself sitting on a lovely silver boat which is formed by a crescent moon. Now you are floating along a river or lake on the energy of the crescent moon, enjoying the creative life. Your boat is carrying you safely from one shore to the next. Simply enjoy yourself!

If your mind wanders from this scene, silently say the mantra *māno-ramam*. *Māno* means "mind," and *ramam* means "player"; the mind-player, the one who dwells within. Be in tune with this beautiful creative energy, this immortal dancer in life.

The function of mantras is to lead you to the deep experience of meditation. When you feel you are in tune with the inner creative force, then let the mantra go. It is like riding an elevator. Let it take you to the floor you want; then get out or it will carry you back to the ground floor again. When you enter the ecstasy of experience, allow all words to remain on the surface.

Now in your meditation, you are relaxing and visualizing the river or lake which pleases you. Be calm and free from any excitement, tension, or haste. Quietly watch the beautiful, flowing water and see yourself and your life floating smoothly on the silver crescent boat. Experience the equanimity from which springs your creative energy. Free yourself from the old ideas and become natural within this serene meditation.

CHAPTER III

Manipura—The Indweller,
Your Hidden Power

Many people think that meditation is an escape from responsibility and participation in the world; but, in reality, it is a process of ascending to a higher level of satisfaction and contentment from which you can realize your life's mission. It is impossible for you to reach this level as long as your consciousness is trapped in the valley of fluctuating desires, greed, insecurity, sensual need, and the drive for power. Whether we realize it or not, our minds are hypnotized by the outer world, captured by these external needs and desires.

If you turn your attention to the innermost quiet recesses of your being, you will discover just how much you are under the influence of the world. Ask yourself, "Am I doing what I do out of genuine need or am I copying others? Do I try to impress others to prove that I am somebody, that I am something special? How often do I continue to do something in order to maintain a certain status although the effort is a burden to me?"

Sometimes we may be torn between the external push toward activity and our internal desire for peace. Our minds continue to prod us toward activity by persuading us that if we don't make a good impression, we will not remain long in this particular circle of friends. Whether or not people are actually paying attention to us, we are convinced that they are watching and judging us, and we indulge in our fear of their opinion.

What can we do or where can we go to free ourselves of this influence? There is one answer, and that is meditation. With the help of meditation, we can touch the core of inner peace, where we are not distracted by our daily concerns—where we can experience a lofty state of being.

In meditation, you become quiet for awhile and untie yourself from the influence of the past, which drags you downward. When you are completely alone with yourself, a hidden energy begins surging upward within you. It will not come if your attention is elsewhere. It is as impossible to experience the surge of energy when your mind is distracted as it is to sing and eat simultaneously. The energy emerges only when you are completely attentive. The ancients used to say that the mind is a slayer of the soul because the undisciplined mind is capable of destroying one's peace and joy and the experience of one's own essence.

As we sit in meditation, we gradually transcend all the layers of society's influence until we reach the highest state of inner clarity. The process is similar to a swimmer who has dived into a pool. His purpose is not to remain forever on the bottom, but to come up to the surface. In the same way, we are slowly rising up from that bottom level of confusion, indecision, and irresponsibility where the mind is in perpetual duality: to do or not to do, to be or not to be, to go or not to go. We must set aside some time each day to quiet the mind and allow the answers we have been groping for to emerge spontaneously.

When the mind is quiet, you can say with conviction, "I want to do it; I am going to do it; it is done." You see the end of the road even before you have started the journey; the task you begin is accomplished already in your mind. It is like traveling somewhere for the second or third time: You know what it will be like to land at the airport; who will meet you; and where they will take you. You enjoy a degree of mental awareness that permits you to see the goal beforehand. In other words, you have learned to rise to that level of awareness which embraces the whole of consciousness. From that level, you can perceive how life is evolving, how things take place.

The first step is to become aware that this body of ours is a combination of four basic elements, which we have called earth, water, fire, and air. Next, we ask ourselves what it is that animates this body so that it moves, speaks, sees, and feels? What is it that, when it departs, leaves the body to stagnate and decompose? One moment there is a beautiful human being who is communicating, planning, managing; and in the next moment, all the planning and communicating is over. What has departed? What is this life and death?

Once when my father and I were celebrating my birthday, he told me he had a little pain. So he lay down with his head in my lap and while I was comforting him, he quietly repeated the mantra, *Om namo arihantānam* ("I bow to those souls who have conquered their inner enemies"). Then he closed his eyes. At that moment, a doctor who was present told me it was over. "What is over?" I asked.

He said, "Your father is dead." Dead? I couldn't understand what had happened, and I felt a little angry. Just one minute before, my father had been alive and, in a moment, he had had a heart attack and was gone.

I later meditated on this incident, which opened the whole mystery of life to me. I saw that while we are thinking and planning everything, we really have no idea who is behind the plan. While we are constantly weaving the cloth of life with so much jealousy, anger, hatred, prejudice, vanity, and disconnected thoughts, we don't really know who is weaving, nor for how long. We have no idea when our play will be over.

In meditation, however, we experience that Self who makes the body live and the senses and the mind function. We are all born for the purpose of getting in touch with that invisible Self.

As I have mentioned, the first step is to understand that the body is comprised of material elements whose nature is to compose and decompose. Next, we must realize that anything which can be composed can be decomposed. Then we begin to differentiate between the composite form which is forever disintegrating and that inner, indestructible energy which has the power to keep these elements composed and revitalized. This energy is the Self, the soul;

[25]

and it is this force which also has the power to heal. At present, we do not know how to heal because we have not seen what lies beyond the material form.

The first center connects us to the element of earth, the same element of which our skin and bones are composed. Our ego, our tendency to identify totally with this earthly body, falls away as it begins to dawn on us that this body is not "mine alone"; it is universal. The body is nothing more than an aggregate of universal particles which the Self has collected to fulfill its mission. When the mission is over, these particles will disperse once more into the universe. The personal "mine" becomes the universal "Thine" as we understand that these particles are collected temporarily for our use. Composing and decomposing is a continuous process that takes place on the level of the physical body; but the Self who composes is never lost. In deep meditation, you will be able to perceive the distinction between the composer and the composed and this insight will bring you a sense of joy which will dispel all fear and anxiety.

This idea is well-illustrated by a story about a musician who had written a beautiful composition. After he had taken his bath one morning, he discovered his pet dog tearing the composition into small pieces. He was so angry that his first impulse was to spank his dog for destroying the manuscript. Now, to make matters worse, a brisk wind blew the little bits of paper out the open window.

This triggered a new idea! "Why should I get angry at my dog?" he thought. "He did not know this composition was something special. For him, it was merely some paper to play with, as I was earlier playing with melody. He may have destroyed the composition, but, after all, he has not destroyed the composer. If I maintain my tranquility, I shall compose again."

In this mood of forgiveness and equanimity, he composed three new pieces that were more brilliant than the first! "Now," he said, smiling, "I have created something truly unique in which there is the essence of the invisible because I am no longer identified with my composition. I am in tune with that composer which survives all that is composed."

This insight is a source of great strength to the aware person because he sees beyond the limits of this form. Knowing that the Self who composes is never destroyed, that "I was, I am, I will be," you are able to allow all feelings of insecurity to drop away. Even the fear of death is transcended with this knowledge. You become free to care for and heal your body—free from the fear of loss or annihilation.

Meditating on the second center, you confront your fear of being uncreative, of being incapable of doing something. You may have noticed that before you initiate something positive, all kinds of negative thoughts spring to mind.

How many people do you know, for example, who fill their suitcases with various types of medicine before they go on a trip "just in case"? Unknowingly, they have brought the sickness with them in their anticipation of illness. Believe it or not, 60 percent of your sickness is in your luggage when you travel and only 40 percent is in the new environment. If you don't take that 60 percent with you, the 40 percent will not affect you very much, especially if you eat and drink sensibly.

In order to overcome the anxiety that some trouble or illness or inner lack will prevent you from accomplishing your goal, focus on the surge of creative energy at the second center. Gradually you will develop a keener sense of purpose and direction. From your new perspective, you will see risks as challenges which call forth your inner store of energy and lead you to realize your full creative potential.

Now you are ready to move to the third point of meditation at the navel, the center of power, expression, and expansion. Just as the mother gives a child to the world, nurturing it for nine months in her womb through the umbilical cord, so, psychologically, we become expansive and giving as we meditate on this center through which we were originally nourished.

Life has two requirements for us: that we commune with the inner Self, and that we communicate with the world. In order to experience true outward communication with society, with friends, and with family, we must first experience deep inner communion with our real nature. One of our obstacles both to our Self-knowledge and to our ability to communicate is the power game of the ego. Ego is contraction. It is the fear of losing something. It is the need to control and manipulate others. Those who try to control others, however, are, in reality, controlled and limited by their own ego trips. When you become in tune with this third center, you break the bonds of this constricting ego and experience a deepening communion with your real nature. Your outward expression will become both expansive and positive.

This center is associated with the element of fire, whose nature is always to move upward radiating light and heat. Yogis in the Himalayan mountains meditate on this fire element, which they call *agni*. Becoming one with it, they protect themselves from the severe cold of winter there. The only difference between the power of those yogis and us is that we allow our intellect to put limits on our idea of the possible. We say, "It cannot happen to me. How can I get warm just by concentrating on fire?"

In reality, however, our thinking profoundly affects our body. Suppose, for instance, someone insults you. Immediately, you will blush and your hands will start to tremble. Look at the change which has come over you as the result of a single insult! See how pale and cold you become when you glimpse something frightening; or when you see your beloved one, feel the thrill of joy passing through your whole body. How do these changes occur? They happen spontaneously because you do not interfere with them when you are engrossed in the experience before you. So allow yourself to feel the power of inner energy and warmth by focusing your attention on the element of fire. It can consume all fluctuating desires, all unpleasant feelings, all accumulated fears.

Sit in a comfortable and relaxed position. Bring your full attention to the area of the navel, which, in Sanskrit, is called *manipura*. *Mani* means "jewel" and *puram* means "city"; that city or place where the bright, precious jewel of inner power is felt. Just as a sparkling jewel radiates brilliant facets of light, so does a flame flicker and burn brightly. Visualize this small flame slowly increasing, sending streaks of red and yellow light higher and higher.

The meditative symbol is a triangle or pyramid; so imagine red and yellow flames reaching ever upward in a pyramid shape, giving off light and heat. One by one, burn those events in your past which continue to haunt you in spite of your having analyzed them. Psychologically, you may have been aware of them; now, spiritually, you can remove them. Use them as fuel for your fire. If anything bothers you during the day, prepare that fire in your imagination and burn it, saying, "All is gone."

An alternative symbol for this center is a wheel (*chakra*), whose spokes radiate outward from its center. Each spoke symbolizes a ray of energy emanating from the core of this circle. Some traditions use this type of symbol for all the energy centers and have specified a particular number of rays for each center. Using this approach, you would visualize for the first center, a wheel of energy having four rays; for the second, a wheel having six rays; for the third, a wheel having ten rays; for the fourth, a wheel having twelve rays; for the fifth, a wheel having sixteen rays; for the sixth, a wheel having sixty-four rays; and for the seventh and last center, a wheel of one thousand rays. I give you this information here so that if you want to experiment with this symbol at some future point in your meditation practice, you will have the precise tools with which to work. You may choose to combine the two methods, placing the symbols I have originally given you within the symbol of a circle. For example, for the third center, you would visualize the pyramid of fire within a circle of energy or light.

Remember, these symbols are simply tools to aid you in focusing the mind. They are your links to a particular quality of energy. Eventually, you will leave all these aids behind as you glide into the full experience of the energy itself.

To begin with, however, it will be most helpful to focus on the purifying element of fire. Imagine the pyramid of red and yellow flames in the area of the navel. Becoming one with this element which has the power to burn away all limitations, feel yourself becoming more and more buoyant and peaceful. Even your sight can be enhanced through focusing on the illuminating aspect of fire.

As you sit quietly in meditation, silently repeat the mantra *rām-rām-rām*, which connects you to the power of the Higher Self. *Rām* means "the indweller who gives life to these senses, mind, and body."

Discover this indweller and be in tune with the power of your inner flame to set you free from all negativity. Break through the ego's tendency to control and manipulate, and experience your real source of strength within. Let your communication with the world reflect the peace and joy which flow naturally from your communion with the inner Self.

CHAPTER IV

Anāhata—Love,
The Ever-Expanding Circle

Meditation is like a ladder: Each rung takes us a little higher until we eventually arrive at the top. First, however, we must see something above us that we want to reach. In the physical world it is easy to determine the height we want to reach and adjust the ladder accordingly. In our life, on the other hand, we are often unable to envision any height, so we naturally neglect using a ladder. The ladder is useful only after we have first come to believe that there is indeed a higher level of awareness and experience awaiting us.

If we are aware of this height and have faith in its value for us, we naturally move toward it. If, however, we don't take it seriously or perhaps don't even realize it is there, then we live a life in time. Time kills us. That is why wise people question why they are here on earth. They ask themselves if there is any mission in life, or if life is merely a question of existing from day to day. The answer is something we must search for and experience for ourselves.

People frequently come to me when they start to question life and say, "I want to see God." I had the same quest many years ago. I would seek out various teachers telling them I was eager to see God, and they would give me lengthy explanations which still left me unsatisfied. Finally, when I approached my last teacher, he smiled and said simply, "You cannot see God unless you become God. God is not an object to be seen with the eye. When you become God, you will see God within. You cannot see something outside unless it exists in you."

What did he mean—become God, then you will know God? In the first place, he meant that wordy explanations cannot replace experience. Words create conflict and misunderstanding. We cannot rely on them to convey our thoughts and feelings precisely. Too often, they bring dispute and separation between people. We must, instead, trust our own inner experience.

In the second place, he meant that until now we have been searching outside ourselves for that which we will find only within. When we expect the outer world to satisfy us, our longings drive us in all directions: from one place to another, from one mission to another, from one job to another, and from one person to another. Each time, we think, "Yes, let me go there!" When we arrive there, however, we say to ourselves, "No, this is not enough. Let me go somewhere else." The search continues. Do we really know what we are searching for? What do we hope to find in the cities, in the mountains, and in the various activities we pursue?

We are like infants who know they are crying for something, but do not know the name of the thing for which they cry. Once in a while in our wanderings, in a moment of silence, we glimpse what we have been searching for and, like the infant who cannot call it by name, we may point to it. It is something innocent and natural which is unaffected by our graying hair and aging bodies—all the external changes. It is the quality of God which dwells in each of us. Unfortunately, few of us recognize this quality in ourselves because our perception is clouded by the somber and often frightening images of God which we have collected over the years.

Primitive man conceived of God as a father who alternately punished and rewarded his children here on earth. If you go to the Vatican today, you will see God depicted in art as such a father, rewarding some of mankind with heaven and punishing others with hell. No matter how modern we may think we are, we are not free of this ancient concept of God. We have woven the thread of our imagination around this idea. Even when we pray, the image suddenly appears before our mental eye and we discover that we pray to no one but the imagined figure.

Someone once asked me what the difference was between prayer and meditation. I told him, "Prayer is when you speak to God whether or not God is listening. Meditation is God speaking to you when you are silent." In meditation, you are calm and receptive. You are like an open door providing a kind of cross ventilation so that the air of divinity can move through you. How can this fresh air of divinity move through you if your door is closed?

There is a beautiful story about Krishna in Indian mythology which illustrates this point very well. Krishna is a god in a particular cult. According to the story, he was especially popular among the young women of his time. He was a very romantic figure who was forever playing a flute. One of the women named Rādhā was so jealous of this flute, which received all of Krishna's time and attention, that she finally snatched it away from him.

"Why do you love this flute so much that it never leaves your lips?" she demanded. "Why don't you pay as much attention to me?"

Krishna smiled, "Because there is nothing inside this flute; it is empty. Whatever breath I breathe into it turns into music. You, on the other hand, are already filled to the brim. I prefer something which is hollow, something which has space within so that it can receive my breath and create beautiful music."

Just as music is created in physical space, so does meditation require psychological space. If we are to experience this breath of divinity, we must remove all the old projections and prejudices which clog our minds and prevent us from recognizing our innate beauty. Our preconceived biases form a mental set of scales by which we continually measure ourselves and the people around us. We are never free of these scales, which inevitably weigh us down and block our happiness.

You may have noticed children who are always smiling and giggling because they are not loaded down with years of accumulated prejudices. They are filled with love and have no idea how to suppress their joy. We also must open ourselves and make room for the fresh air to pass through.

[35]

That is why we do not address anyone in meditation; we simply resound with the vibrations of our inner music. Becoming God, we experience God.

Throughout history, all the great teachers have told us, "The kingdom of heaven is within you. Do not search outside. That kingdom is waiting for you within. Come and be here." We are now learning to climb the ladder of awareness so we can reside in that pure state of consciousness which is the kingdom of heaven within.

As we climb higher and higher, we remain in tune with nature, with the cosmos. That is why we first focus on the earth center, building a foundation of security. We realize that fear has no independent reality; it is a product of the mind and the emotions, which tend to magnify things out of proportion.

With the mantra *shivam shānti*, we replace fear with feelings of peace and benediction. Each meditation reminds us that life itself is a blessing. It is enough just to awaken in the morning and see the sun shining and know you are alive. The joy of living should not depend on having an expensive car or many acres of land or someone to live with. If these outer things come to you, enjoy them; but do not feel rejected and depressed without them. Life is simply being alive and waking up to a new day. It is looking forward to saying hello to a friend, someone out of so many millions of people to whom you can talk freely. It is being able to love with an undemanding heart.

Once I watched a little girl tenderly taking care of her small doll. First she prepared a bed for it and laid it gently on the bed. Then she carefully covered it because it was winter. Finally, when her doll was asleep, she slept. She did all these things with such care and tenderness, not because she expected some appreciation from the doll, but simply because she was happy to care for it.

Have you ever thought about this kind of love? Have you ever loved somebody without expectations just because you wanted to love? What would you do if it were your birthday and your loved one forgot to bring you a gift? Would you be patient and understanding, knowing that the spirit of the day is in your own heart, not in satisfying your expectations of how others should act? Or, would you berate your lover, saying, "Why don't you appreciate me? Why haven't you brought me a gift? What kind of lover are you?"

I do not mean to imply that one should neglect expressing one's love. Just now I am not referring to the person who forgot the gift, but to the one who expected it. This is a small example of the way our expectations spoil our days. If someone has forgotten to note your birthday or some other special occasion, you may remind him or her gently. Let him realize that it is all right that he forgot. You may say, "Whether or not you bring me a gift is not important between us. It is we ourselves who are important." Next time, your friend will remember and will return your love and consideration twofold.

Love flows freely when people sense that there is no demand on them. You must be like the little girl with her doll. Allow your love to flow unconditionally toward someone close to you. That person may be young or old, your child, your parent, or your friend. It makes no difference. Your love is the natural expression of feeling alive.

Let us start each day with this vibrant, loving feeling. At present, life is a burden to many of us because we are dependent on external things for our satisfaction. We struggle for wealth and success and when they are not forthcoming, we ask, "What is the meaning of life? Why do I live?" We exist, but we do not really experience life. These external achievements are nothing next to knowing what life is. Once we realize this fact, we will stop fabricating our own misery. We will no longer be the slaves of an unruly imagination which grasps after ephemeral things. Instead, we will be secure in the certain knowledge that we are happy and will remain so.

Why are we living? If we thrill with life, that is reason enough. People spend thousands of dollars to prolong their lives. Even in their final days, they are striving to live one hour longer. Yet how many days have already passed by them unnoticed? Hundreds of days have come and gone. So, it is time we begin paying attention to each day and reminding ourselves of the miracle that we are alive and breathing. The whole world is lying before us, and we are free to do what we want with our lives.

Wise people, who have educated their minds and become inwardly independent, are able to inspire others to live fully as they do. When you become truly alive, you will not have to find friends; they will seek you out no matter where you are. I hear from people I haven't seen for ten years or more. They write me from all over the world, including Russia, where people assume that there is no religion. I am amazed that these people have not forgotten our moments together after so much time.

What do you think it is that makes us remember someone and want to communicate with him again? We respond to the good feeling which flows naturally from that person who is emotionally self-sufficient. Meditating on the first energy center with the mantra *shivam shānti* will help you to establish this sense of self-sufficiency and vitality.

When you have absorbed this peaceful benediction, turn your attention to the second center. Here, indecision gives way to certainty. What you determine to do, you do. The doubt which drains your energy and prevents you from accomplishing your chosen task is merely a weakness of the mind which can be overcome. Everyone possesses a hidden creative potentiality which is activated by belief in oneself. All it needs is the right moment to call it forth.

I'll give you a good example: There was a man in Bombay who became gravely ill. One day his son came to me and persuaded me to visit his father. When I saw the old man, he was too weak to move. It took two nurses to help him from his bed. Several days later, I read in the newspaper that a fire had broken out in the building in which he lived. This man was living on the seventh floor and there were no elevators, so I assumed that it would not have been possible to save him. Then, to my surprise, someone told me that this old man had been the first person to escape. While all the other tenants were gathering their belongings, he rushed ahead of them down the stairs.

After a few days, I visited him especially to verify the story. Again I found him lying in bed with two nurses attending him. "How could you climb down seven flights of stairs in your condition?" I asked him.

"I don't know," he said. "God sent me the energy."

Then I told him, "No, God did not send the energy; the crisis did. We always have that energy, but we are generally unaware of it. At the right moment, the energy bursts forth."

Each of us possesses infinite energy which surges out at the right moment like the force of an atom when it is split. We learn how to tap that energy in its different aspects by meditating on these seven centers. With the first three centers, we have been focusing specifically on the connection between the microcosm and the macrocosm. We have been strengthening our sense of security and creativity and burning the limiting, negative habits of thought which prevent us from experiencing our innate vitality.

Now, at the fourth center, the heart, we experience love. Love is a beautiful, divine element in the universe which brings people together and initiates communication. When you begin to feel real love, you will discover that the world is a wonderful place in which to dwell. You will feel love for everyone regardless of color, background, or form. One's life is such a short journey, why spoil the precious experience of love with demands and criticism? Conditional love cannot last long.

Instinctively you know you cannot change anyone with criticism and conditions. You must learn instead to accept each individual as he or she is, just as you expect to be accepted as you are. If someone attempts to change you, chances are you will be the first to object. Why not demand the same standard of acceptance from yourself? If you cannot remain happily in someone's company, simply allow that person to leave without trying to mould or manipulate him. That which you don't like about this person may be a lesson for his growth.

For example, one man who often came to see me in India was a chain smoker. He was also in very poor health. I felt such compassion for him, I urged him to give up smoking. "It is impossible!" he said. "The craving for cigarettes is too deeply ingrained in me. I am miserable without them."

I told him, in that case, to go ahead and smoke and not be embarrassed about it. He should not force himself to give them up on my account. He was concerned that my feelings would be hurt if he didn't follow my advice. "Why should I be hurt? I accept you just as you are whether you smoke or not," I answered. "Smoking is not my problem; it is yours. I only thought that it might be the cause of your present weak condition. That's all!"

Recently, I met this man again and noticed he was not smoking. Out of curiosity, I asked him about it and he said he had dropped the habit two years before. I was astonished! "You once told me that you could live without your wife, but not without your cigarettes. What happened to you?" I asked.

Then he answered, "The doctor told me my cigarettes were leading to cancer and I already had the symptoms. When I left the Bombay Hospital, I took my cigarettes and my lighter out of my pocket and threw them into the garbage. From that moment, I gave up smoking." Then, as an afterthought, he asked me why I had not been more forceful with him. Why had I not demanded that he stop smoking?

"If," I said, "I had ordered you to stop smoking, you may have followed my advice, but the desire would have remained. You would always have believed that I had compelled you not to smoke and eventually you would have resented me. Now you have given it up freely of your own will because of your personal experience."

In life, there is no need for us to be upset because others do not do what we think is best for them. We must accept them as they are; we must watch and wait and love. The time will come when they will learn directly from their own experience.

Love is acceptance, and acceptance means giving the people around us room in which to live, to ponder, to learn. Acceptance allows for the natural blossoming of understanding. We must be careful not to suffocate our partner or our friend with the bondage of a conditional love. That kind of love stifles growth, and the relationship becomes stagnant and unrewarding.

What is the nature of real love and what happens to us and to our lives when we are touched by it? First, consider breath. We cannot live without it; yet if we try to hold on to it, we die of suffocation. Love is our spiritual breath. We cannot live and thrive without it; but if we try to grasp it, it withers and so do we. As we inhale and exhale, inhale and exhale, we are receiving and giving not only air, but the breath of love from the universe. Therefore, when you meditate on the fourth center, the heart, first take time to be aware of the element of air which is fresh and ever-moving within and around you. As you become relaxed and light, feel your awareness expanding into the whole universe. When you connect with the life around you through the heart, your love will flow both in reverence toward those who have realized their perfection more fully than you have and in benevolent service to your fellow beings who are in need on the path of life.

This fourth center of meditation is called *anāhata*, which, in Sanskrit, means "that which is ever-new; that which is constantly resounding without being struck; that which is self-sustaining." As the heart beats continuously, renewing and sustaining the physical body, so too does real love sustain and refresh us spontaneously without outside stimulus. It is ever-flowing.

The symbol for this center is a perfect circle, a zero point, a beautiful dot of light. You may picture this circle as a lovely, transparent, blue color—sky blue. Now, slowly enlarge this small, blue dot of light until it fully embraces you, the people around you, the whole family of man, and, finally, all life in the universe. This ever-expanding circle is the inner touch of the heart called love.

Next, link the mantra *sohum* to the breath; inhale *so* and exhale *hum*. Connecting this mantra to the physical breath will help you to be in tune with the spiritual breath of love. *So* literally means "That" and *hum* means "I am." What is meant by "That"? It is our other, higher Self—it is that which is beautiful, that which is perfect, that pure Self within. Whatever you admire as beautiful and perfect in someone else exists in you also; otherwise, you would not be able to perceive it. Experiencing this truth, you become truly self-sufficient, no longer demanding anything from anyone. You are able to accept each person just as he is. When you discover in your own heart that which you admire in others, you will understand that our quest is not to see God as we might see something which is separate from us. We can find and experience in our own selves the perfection we call God; but, for this, we must expand the scope and refine the quality of our love.

Start by perceiving the whole world as your lover. Let any idea that people are against you fall away. The whole world is for you. Even those who criticize you do you a service; they are your teachers. Pain itself is your teacher; it breaks your attachments and the addictions which bind you. Each painful event brings new depth of understanding, so do not run away even from pain. Feel it, watch it, study its source and the meaning it has for you and you will come away from your pain with profound knowledge. You will touch upon the real and the permanent behind the unreal and the temporary. When you perceive your real Self, your love will be the bridge between you and your fellow beings.

Meditating on the fourth center will help you to begin loving yourself and experiencing the whole of life as love. You will be able to wake up each morning and say, "I am happy simply because I love myself and I am fully alive!" The whole spiritual journey starts from this point because love is the foundation of all spiritual teaching.

Love is the universal cycle of perfection. It is the zero point which leads to infinity. It is a single drop of water expanded into an infinite ocean.

CHAPTER V

Vishuddha—Abundance, Experiencing the Limitless

My teacher used to tell a story of a learned young man who had read in the scriptures that there existed a marvelous and precious stone. He who held this stone in his possession would be free of all worry. As soon as the young man read this, he left home in search of this wonderful prize. For fifty years, he journeyed throughout the world in vain. Finally, exhausted by his travels, he returned home an old and disappointed man of eighty. Then one day as he was resting on the bank of a river by his home, he noticed a stone sparkling at the water's edge. When he examined it more carefully, he realized to his astonishment that this was the very stone for which he had searched all his life. What could he do now with such a remarkable gift? He was an old man near the end of his days and he had spent his life searching the world for that which awaited him at his own doorstep.

These seven centers are points of meditation which will lead us to the prize at our own doorstep—to the inner source of happiness, harmony, and strength, the source of all those things for which we truly yearn. Like the man in the story, we already have this wonderful prize but we do not know it.

The purpose of each meditation is to understand the essence, the special quality, of each energy or experience. If you feel peace, security, creativity, you have reached the goal of the meditation. Do not be disturbed if you have difficulty visualizing. These visual images are simply tools or symbols to help focus the mind; they are not the goals of the meditation.

In reality, meditation is for training this mind. The soul itself does not need it. It is already omnipotent, omnipresent, and omniscient. The mind, on the other hand, is conditioned and limited by accumulated attitudes. It creates duality in us and we find ourselves doing things we aren't happy about. The unfocused mind is unclear and paranoid; it alienates us from the world around us.

Meditation on these seven centers brings your mind to one-pointedness. These centers are like a map or blueprint. You know that before you construct a house, you must have an outline of it so that the entire house exists ahead of time on paper. Now, looking at this blueprint, you can change any detail to suit you better before you begin construction. The outline indicates how the finished product will look and how you should go about constructing it. At this stage, it is like a children's game of make-believe. However, to enjoy living in a real house, you must go further than make-believe; you must labor to build it. The symbols of the centers are our outline, our meditative blueprint on which we concentrate our attention in order to reach the reality behind the symbol. Like the builder, we must not stop at the blueprint, but go beyond it. We must learn and practice and grow until we experience real change in ourselves. Learning and practice go hand in hand.

The self-confidence you derive from meditation will be reflected in a new feeling of confidence in you by your family, friends, and co-workers. Whether you realize it or not, the subtle vibrations you emanate are inevitably communicated to the people around you. You receive from others what you have already created within your own self. In other words, what you give comes back. Your inner security will create security in others.

With continued practice, meditation will gradually replace your self-doubt with renewed creative inspiration. This force will be felt continuously in all your actions so long as you keep reminding yourself of it. Meditation is not only for twenty short minutes a day—it is to be carried over into the whole day. If you find it difficult to keep the object of meditation in the back of your mind, I suggest you make a note on a small index card for each center of meditation. Carry one of these cards with you in your pocket or purse. Now, just as you check the mirror to see if you look outwardly presentable, glance at the card to see if all is in order inside. Creativity is inevitable when the outer and inner worlds are in order, but it takes time to change a lifetime of habits which have become firmly rooted in us. Growth and change will occur naturally if you are consistent in your practice.

*   *   *

Now we approach the fifth center, located in the throat area at the larynx. This center is called *vishuddha*, which means "Pure amidst all purity and Holy amongst the holiest." *Vishuddha* is the center of abundance and space. As we let go all impure elements—all resentments, anger, and bitterness—we are set free to enjoy the boundless reaches of space. Everything is available to the one who is pure.

To connect with this feeling of unlimited space and plenty, first spend two or three minutes focused on the heart center. The fourth and fifth centers are closely connected because love and space are like two sides of a coin. Love thrives where there is space, when we are not bombarded and constricted by ephemeral desires and petty jealousies and demands. Those who know the meaning of real love do not attempt to possess love, for they know that it would be like trying to grasp space. The moment they close their fingers around it, they are left empty-handed.

First, therefore, sit alone and relaxed, holding your attention on the inner dot of light. Remember, this point of light is Love. Now, begin enlarging this point of love and, as it continues expanding, remind yourself, "This is my True Self which does not want to hate anybody. When I am reconciled with those whom I have hated, I will be happy because I shall have come to my True Self." *So* is your real Self, your highest Self, and *hum* is "I am," the created self or form. Let the true Self be expressed in this created form. As you repeat the mantra *sohum,* know that anything outside the real Self is mental conditioning which can be undone. You can unravel that which you have woven wrongly and reweave the fabric of your mind to harmonize with your real Self.

What, previously, you took to be your real self—depression, dependence, resentment, anger, insecurity, unhappiness—are, in fact, not the real Self. The real Self is Love. In the past, your awareness of this Higher Self has often been obscured by the rage and resentment which are part of the unreal, part of the borrowed mental programs and expectations. To uncover the Real within, you must take the time to dive deep into your inner being. Nobody is going to do it for you. You must make the effort yourself.

In your meditation, begin to let go all the ill feelings you are harboring toward anyone. It may be helpful sometimes to visualize a blackboard on which you mentally write the names of anyone you resent or dislike. If you find it difficult to visualize, then write the names on a piece of paper. Now, gradually go deep, deep into yourself and for each name examine how and where and why this resentment started. Did it start with some thoughtless words? Was it the result of your projection or misinterpretation? Perhaps you had expected something from someone and in your disappointment, anger and bitterness were born. Perhaps you heard second- or third-hand that someone had spoken against you and you took it to heart and now you are estranged from that person. In so many, many ways we have become alienated from the people around us and carry the burden of our resentments in our minds.

As you probe deeper into your memory, you will suddenly realize that you have bound yourself to the very people you have disliked. Anger and resentment tie you to the object of your anger so that you are not free to move forward. I have seen people experience the heights of joy and moments of the most serene meditation only to return to the same state from which they started. They are like boats moored to the shore. A breeze may twist and turn them, but you know they are not going anywhere. They are weighted down. People who have not loosed themselves from their resentments cannot enjoy progress. No matter where they go, they always come back to the same place.

It is a common belief that finding love is a matter of luck; but, I tell you, it is rather a question of tying and untying. The moment we untie ourselves from our resentments, we are able to allow love to blossom. Those whose hearts are free of animosity will not lack friends. They may not always find lovers, but they will surely enjoy loving friendship. The West has a tendency to confuse lust with love. People tend to hide their lust under the guise of love, but this is a distortion. Real love has nothing to do with lust; it is an understanding and communication between people which overcomes any apparent boundaries of age or background.

When I was a child of four and five years old, my good friend was an old man of sixty-five. I could bring all my problems to him and he would always give me a right, honest answer. One day when I was four years old, my mother died. I couldn't understand where she had gone and why she hadn't returned, so I went to this old man and asked him where she was. It was evening and he pointed out the moon and the stars to me. "Your mother has gone to heaven where she can enjoy all those beautiful stars!" he said.

This old man gave me a new understanding. Everyone

else had simply said she was dead and would never come back. I looked up at the stars and the moon and I thought, "Yes! Everything is bright and sparkling, and she is happy! How can my mother come back soon when she is in such a beautiful place?" This old man was a great help to me. We had our own language, our own special communication. He could express things in such a way as to lead me to new insights.

Love can be shared with someone of any race or social position or age because love is a coming together on a level beyond all these external labels. Love is communication between souls—between my real Self and your real Self. The artificial self, which is forever fluctuating between exhilaration and depression, drops away as you focus on the real Self—that ever-expanding, universal love.

Now, moving from the fourth to the fifth center, visualize a scarlet or mauve oval. Gradually expand the space within the oval, breaking all barriers until it is without limitation. Feel that now all energy is available to you. Whenever your mind becomes distracted, use the mantra *aim*,* which is Sanskrit for "the energy of wisdom, the energy of plenty and purity." In time, you will begin to experience purity as synonomous with space, with abundance, and with wisdom.

At this point in working on the seven centers, many people find it helpful to practice *prāna yāma* breathing. To do this, alternately block one nostril with the thumb and the other with the third finger. Using the ratio 1:4:2, inhale

---

* Pronunciation is similar to the English "aim."

through one nostril, hold the breath, and exhale through the other nostril. For example, based on this ratio, breathe in through your right nostril to the count of 4, then retain the breath for 16 counts, and exhale through the left nostril, counting 8. Wait approximately 15 seconds and repeat the exercise, inhaling through the left nostril and exhaling through the right. Later, according to your capacity, you may increase the number of counts you breathe and retain the breath based on the ratio I have given you.

This breathing exercise practiced at the start of your meditation is an excellent technique for taking oxygen deep into the lungs and into all the blood cells, and releasing the carbon dioxide from the body. It is also useful for calming and focusing the mind. When you have completed this exercise (inhale, retain, exhale) five times, continue with your meditation, feeling your inner purity as you expand into universal space.

Those who meditate on this center will begin to hear the subtle resonance of the universal sound as their sense of hearing becomes increasingly keen. As the first center is connected with the sense of smell; the second, with the sense of taste; the third, with the sense of sight; and the fourth, with the sense of touch; so the fifth center will refine our sense of hearing.

Focusing on your energy at the throat, you will find that your words have a new authority. The same words which were previously rejected by others will now be welcomed by the listening ear. Why? Because the energy behind them will have changed. You will know exactly when, why, and how to speak. You will know when to keep silent. Being in tune with the essence of space, you will offer space to those around you and they will appreciate it. You will be speaking from the realm of purity and truth, and those who listen will recognize it. The one whose hand is no longer grasping and clinging is open to receive the bounty of the universe. Now, at the fifth center, that person is you.

CHAPTER VI

Ājnā—The Eye
of Inner Wisdom

How does one get away from the endless repetition of daily existence? Day after day, year after year, we get up in the morning, bathe, eat, drink, take the car out of the garage or wait for the bus, go to work, return home, and so on. We have repeated these same activities twenty, a hundred, a thousand—innumerable—times until they all seem nothing more than part of a monotonous effort for survival. People are bored, tired of themselves. Why? How can we transform a tedious existence into the vivid, joyful experience of life?

If we reserve some time to be alone with ourselves and delve into the depths of our being, we will begin to catch glimpses of that higher Self. These glimpses reveal our inner evolution, our gradual upward movement. Then life is worth living because we see that we are not merely getting by, that we are growing toward that perfection which we have glimpsed.

We are all on the spiritual path for the purpose of understanding where we are going and what we are in the process of creating. The centers are an indication of the various manifestations of our energy. The symbols used in our meditations are not empty forms. Each can be a powerful link between our minds and the essence of the particular aspect of energy on which we are concentrating. When we are calm and in harmony with the meditation, these symbols open our inner door so that we may enter into the different ecstasies of life. Being in tune with each center is like having the right key for the right lock and knowing just how to slide the key into the lock so that it fits exactly and the door opens.

If you give these symbols to someone who does not understand their meaning, he will say you are wasting your time. What does this person know of the true experience of meditation? He is like someone who, standing before a closed door with the right key in his hand, is nevertheless unable to adjust the position of the key within the lock so that the door will open. He has both the proper key and the proper lock, but not the proper connection.

If you really connect with a center, its energy will help you change your life. Inner growth is not a question of how much information you have acquired but of how much you have practiced. It is similar to eating. You benefit not from how much food you have taken into your mouth, but from how much you are actually able to digest. Yet, there are people who never stop eating. They continually stuff themselves without even taking the time to chew properly until their digestive system finally breaks down. Similarly, in our spiritual growth, progress does not depend on how much knowledge we have or how many books we read, but on experience itself.

I have seen people who have read the contents of an entire library; but when I look at their lives, I see that they are in turmoil. These people do not know how to communicate, how to live. What good is all that reading if it does not teach them how to order their lives?

There truly is wisdom in the old proverb "Practice makes perfect." Why do you think no one has written instead, "Reading makes a man perfect"? Reading has no value unless it connects with one's experience. Without this connection, people read indiscriminately. They are driven in a hundred directions by contradictory viewpoints. One opposing thought is superimposed upon another until all their energy is canceled out.

For this reason, we have the tradition in India of remaining steadily with one teacher whose calm disposition, clear thinking, and compassionate heart set an example for the student. Whenever the student has some difficulty, he consults his teacher. There is no conflict. The energy which might have been wasted on contradictory ideas is channeled into the student's growth until his life becomes harmonious.

I have never seen anything more corroding than inner conflict. Once the seed of doubt is planted in the mind, it begins to absorb all one's energy. Eventually, the body itself is affected. Illness starts in the mind with our conflicts, prejudices, jealousies, and passions. Knowing this, wise people select that path, that life-style, which is conducive to their growth and tranquility. They take care to create a pleasant atmosphere and seek out the proper guidance. They couple their learning with practice. We, too, must use discrimination so that we do not consume our energy in useless confusion. There must be some direction in our study. We must strive to transform what we learn intellectually into real experience.

This transformation takes place through the process of meditation. Therefore, as you focus your attention on each center, let the symbols and mantras lead you to the energy itself. Experience that energy.

When you turn your attention to the fifth center, you see an oval form which gives you an outline of space. Ultimately, you transcend the form and go into that energy of space. You experience space itself. Having space within you, you give space—physical, mental, and emotional space —to the life around you. If someone has the urge to say something, you let him speak. Give him space. Once he has spoken, he has emptied himself of what he needed to say; so, now he has room to hear your insights. His heart and mind will be receptive to your words because you have created a space for them in him.

When you force your opinions on people without giving them space to express their own ideas and concerns, your words bounce back at you, causing you pain. People often come to me complaining that no one understands them. Then, I ask, "Have you allowed others to understand you? Have you given them time to digest what you had to tell them or did you go on pouring out your opinions? Have you allowed them to speak also? Did your words come from the heart, from love? Or did they come from your own projection, your particular bias?"

As I have told you before, love and space are partners. Your words will not collide and wrestle with each other if you have made room for them with your love. When you have something to say, see that it comes from your heart center. If you speak instead from your particular bias, your words will surely be rejected because they do not carry the real essence of truth. They are colored by that level of thinking from which you are speaking—by your anger or jealousy or whatever. You may have noticed that as soon as you speak in anger, the person who is listening also becomes angry. He hears only your anger, not what you are trying to say. Your anger has ignited his anger which, in turn, bounces back to you. It becomes a vicious circle.

How difficult it is to control anger and transform it into love! Yet, that is precisely what you must do if you are to communicate something meaningful to others. Remember that, "To err is human, to forgive is divine." Your anger can be dissolved by your own forgiveness.

Words travel anywhere and everywhere in the universe, in space. Astronauts speak from the moon, and ground control receives their message here on earth. There is no barrier. Similarly, nothing but our own anger or abruptness prevents our words from traveling through space into somebody's heart. To be heard, we must reestablish our connection with one another by centering ourselves in love.

Silence plays an important part here. Use it to deal with any inner negative element which prevents your communication. Remain silent. Don't utter a word unless you feel love. When you are able to speak with love, you will surely be heard; for then, one heart will be speaking to another. Both will be in harmony because they are once more connected in love and space.

If you become truly in tune with this center, you will be overwhelmed with friends wherever you go. The whole world will be a houseful of friends and you will enjoy an abundance of love.

The mantra *aim* links you to the vibration of wisdom which evolves out of this love. There is a profound difference between knowledge of the mind and wisdom of the heart. Wisdom is born out of that heart which is ripe and complete. That is why words spoken with love contain truth. That is why they travel through space unimpeded and are welcomed by the listening heart. Now we can see the connection in the fifth center between space, truth, speech, and hearing.

Meditation is not, as some people believe, a word with some far-away esoteric meaning irrelevant to our practical, daily existence. Meditation is a process by which you can transform your whole life-style. It reveals to you your inner weaknesses and helps you to convert them into positive strengths. As you work on the fourth and fifth centers, you gradually resolve all disputes and open up a space for friendship and understanding. Your practice will bring the fruit of your meditation into your environment and into all your relationships. You will be dipped in love. This is the way we have to build the world around us—dipped in love.

* * *

Now we come to the sixth center, called *ājnā,* which means "command." *Ājnā* is the third eye, the eye of inner awareness, the eye of control. It is located in the center of the brow.

This eye of wisdom works in two ways: First, it controls your incoming thoughts; and second, it commands your outgoing thoughts and, ultimately, your words and actions. Ordinarily, thoughts come whether you like it or not. It is difficult to control them. Suppose, for example, you want to sleep, but your thoughts will not leave you alone. They invade your mind from all directions until they seem to fill up your whole bedroom. Meanwhile, you are tossing and turning in your bed, powerless to stop them. Now you can put an end to the influx of thoughts by meditating on the third eye.

Visualize in the center of your brow the symbol of an eye in a beautiful orange color. Watch this eye of command opening and closing, opening and closing. Connect your thoughts with this opening and closing of the third eye. When it is open, you are saying "yes" to your thoughts, and they come to you; but when it is closed, you are saying "no," and the thoughts are stopped. Gradually, you learn not only how, when, and where to use thoughts, but also when not to use them at all. It is like learning to drive a car. One must know not only how to drive it, but also when and how to put on the brakes.

We all have two physical eyes which link us to the outside world. These eyes connect us to the horizontal plane of external appearance. As we all know, appearance is often deceptive; it is incomplete information. The third eye is the vertical eye of wisdom which connects us to the vertical plane of divinity. If we want to see reality, our two physical eyes must work in harmony with the third eye. In other words, we must see not only appearance, but also what lies behind it.

The horizontal plane is narrow and limited whereas the vertical is infinite. If we live only in the horizontal realm, we are caught in the humdrum of daily existence. When we are connected with the vertical, the infinite, we bring new meaning and purpose to our life in the world. As long as we cling to the horizontal plane, we are trapped in our small ego. We are engulfed by our ambitions and anxieties. When we embrace the vertical plane, we transcend our limitations and enter the world of unlimited possibility. Then there is no split between the two, between horizontal and vertical. There is a blend of both. We live in the world, but we are connected to the divine. We see beyond appearance; we are in touch with infinite meaning.

Your sense of self-control will come from the ability to command your thinking process. Whatever happens in the world is a manifestation of thought. You create your world, choosing the people and circumstances around you through the attraction of thought. Therefore, if you want to change your world, you must first change your thought, your inner mechanism for creating your outer world.

Presently, we are under the impression that our external circumstances govern us, causing both our happiness and our misery. In reality, this outer realm is merely the trigger which calls forth whatever is already lying hidden in our inner thought world. Our inner weaknesses prevent us from discerning this subtle process and detecting those out-side influences which activate our negative or positive responses. We can't see that the true cause of our joy and sadness is our inner state of being.

The energy flowing from this inner world is intrinsically neutral, but in our lives now it is manifested both positively and negatively. How we use this inner power determines the quality of its manifestation. It is like electricity. Electricity is simply energy which can be converted to light, to heat, to refrigeration. In other words, its apparent characteristics change depending upon how we channel it. The question is: How do we employ our energy? Learning to master our thoughts enables us to use our energy, our innate talent, positively, so that we consciously harness and direct this inner force.

When you have felt the commanding quality of this center, silently begin to repeat the mantra *pragnā*. It means "inner awareness." *Pragnā* is experienced as ripened wisdom, which is cultivated through the perception of the third eye.

From this height of awareness at the sixth center, this tower of observation, you can view all your actions and re-actions. The five centers you have been studying are now under your gaze, and you can begin to watch when your love turns to lust, when you are motivated by the power drive, what gives rise to your anxieties, and when your inner space contracts. You are your own observer. You see the whole world as a cosmic stage on which you are an actor performing the drama of life. It is your mission to make this play as harmonious, as beautiful, and as meaningful as possible.

Naturally, there will be critics who will want to review your performance. From this center, you can accept both their praise and their criticism with equanimity. You know you must play this drama lightheartedly. After all, what was deadly serious to you in one season of life seems unimportant to you in another. So why should you be somber and inhibited in your acting? Why lose your real identity in the roles you play? Why spoil the drama with tension?

Most people have no idea what they are really doing in life. They identify totally with the process of gain and loss, fame and shame. They do not see that their minds are under the influence of the outer world of changing opinion. In time, this influence crystallizes into psychological conditioning—set patterns of thought—so that people lose touch with the core of their being. They lose touch with the real experience and do not taste the freshness of each moment of life.

We cannot avoid the influence of the world, but we can liberate ourselves from the bondage of identification with it. Normally, by the end of every day, we have retained in our consciousness some residue of the world's influence. This residue surfaces in our dreams at night. We have stored so much of this residue in our consciousness over the years that our centers have become blocked. Burdened by our fears and anger, we lose spontaneity in our life.

It is time we cleared our mental slate. The process of meditation lifts the cloud of confusion and dissolves our crystallized conditioning so that we can perceive the world and ourselves with a new clarity. The light of awareness will transform our thoughts and emotions. It will transmute our self-destructive patterns of behavior into positive, creative enjoyment of life. Even our metabolism will reflect the change in us. Remember that no one enjoys life more fully than the person who is aware.

I have mentioned visualizing the third eye as a brilliant orange color; however, many meditators prefer to imagine a whole spectrum of changing colors. As the five centers are seen from the sixth center of wisdom, so are all their colors, like the rays of a rainbow, within the perception of the third eye. Discover for yourself which method is most helpful in bringing you a sense of clarity, equanimity, and command.

Now, as you meditate on this sixth center, remind yourself not to take your role in life too seriously. Play your part with a light heart so that at the end of each day, you may give yourself a pat on the back and say, "Good show! You played your part very well today!"

CHAPTER VII

Sahasrāra—Pure
Consciousness of Self

The higher we climb, the more panoramic is our view. We are able to see from a height things which are not visible to us from some lower vantage point. This is true in the physical world and on the spiritual plane as well. Height changes our perspective.

You may find it impossible to share what is now within your new range of vision from the sixth and seventh centers with people who still live from the viewpoint of the first energy center. Their scope is limited to the accumulation of possessions and to finding security in material things. Your talk is meaningless to them now. They cannot relate to what you are saying because they are dwelling in the basement and your view is from the top floor, from a higher level of awareness.

You will discover that many things are visible to you now that were unknown to you when you, also, were dwelling in the basement. You will experience life differently as a result.

For instance, the doubt which once engulfed you will have evaporated. That does not mean that from time to time it will not reappear; but it will be slight, and you will have the power to deal with it. From your new outlook, you can see where all the old habits of negative thinking come from, and you can say to yourself with conviction, "This doubt is the old way of thinking and I won't go along with it!" You will have tapped into your source of inner strength.

Your addiction to lust will now diminish as your ability to love increases. You will no longer have the need to bind someone to you, but will be able to allow and encourage his or her freedom.

When you love from your heart, those people around you who are closed begin noticing the difference in you. They start to question their own state of mind, their own emotional blocks. They will wonder why, in the presence of such a free outpouring of love, they remain so closed. Your genuine love will be the catalyst for their opening.

Even your physical well-being is enhanced by your love because love is your natural state. On the other hand, the dark emotions of hatred, depression, and jealousy sap your energy, destroy your inner peace and joy, and bring on illness.

In meditation, you see the oneness of the universe. You no longer emphasize the outward differences between people because you are acutely aware of your unity with them. Seeing yourself in others, you endeavor to live in such a way as to make them comfortable in your presence.

With the sixth center, the inner eye of wisdom is opened.

I have talked to you before about the two physical eyes through which we all gaze into the physical world, the world of changing forms. These eyes reveal only the ephemeral characteristics of one's outer frame—rich and poor, tall and short, and so on. The inner eye, however, perceives the permanent reality behind the temporary form. It sees that nameless traveler who is born into the world, acquires a name, travels the course of life, and departs leaving the name behind. This insight changes your thought patterns. Problems which once loomed very large in your mind are not so intimidating now. The problems have not become any smaller, but you have become bigger in relation to them because you now have in your command a vast reservoir of power. You are connected to the permanent reality behind the passing form. Problems seemed insurmountable when you saw them through a veil of fear and insecurity; but now that you are free of these limitations, you perceive with the clear eye of wisdom.

Seeing ourselves in a new light, we discover that we have a mission in life: to receive divinity and to share that divinity with our fellow beings. Until now, many of us have confined ourselves to a very limited circle of interest. We have thought only in terms of *my* nation, *my* community, *my* group, *my* religion, or, even on a more limited scale, *my* house, *my* family, *my* children, *my* money, *my* car.

For many of us, our happiness depends solely on our children. If they acknowledge us and our efforts on their behalf, we are pleased, we are in heaven. On the other hand, one careless word from them and we are in hell. Why have we built so much attachment to these children? Why have we narrowed our affections to such an extent that our peace of mind depends on their response to us? As our children become mature, why do we insist on giving them what they do not want? Consider carefully what we are really doing.

In reality, we are giving, not to our children, but to ourselves in order to support our attachment. We have labeled a human being "my daughter" or "my son," and concentrated all our generosity on that person. Why? Because he or she is stamped with our particular label. We give because that person carries our surname. We forget that these children do not belong to us. Ultimately, they must lead their own lives. They have their own mission to fulfill.

Meditating on the sixth center brings about a radical change in our understanding so that we no longer think as the majority does. We adopt a new outlook which puts us in touch with the whole of life. Now, we can look beyond the confines of family, community, religion, and nationality. Now, we can say with ease, "Why do I not accept all mankind as my children? There are so many children I am not doing anything for. There are so many people in the world who are in need. Why should I impose on my children who are not ready to receive from me?"

When we refuse to relate beyond the bounds of family or nationality, we ultimately clash with our fellowman. War and exploitation inevitably follow such limited focus. Through meditation, however, we learn to see all living beings as our brothers and sisters.

This brotherhood of mankind must be more than lip

service to a fine ideal; it must be deeply experienced. We must not forget that we live, thanks to universal help. Consider the clothes you wear, the food you eat, everything you use in your day-to-day life. Where did all these things come from? Who harvested the grain and constructed your house? How many farmers and weavers and carpenters have contributed to your comfort? We do not know whose hands have helped us. As you meditate on the sixth center, remind yourself of this with the following thought, "I am living with universal help; so, let me, in my turn, be universal. Let me give to the universe."

Someone once asked Buddha if he could convey his teaching in two words and he said, "Wisdom and compassion." When he was asked to condense his teaching into just one word, he replied, "Wisdom." The Sanskrit word he chose was *pragnā*, the wisdom of the third eye; because he knew that compassion would flow naturally from that man or woman whose perception was all-embracing, universal.

When you attain this level of understanding, all division between "mine" and "thine" disappears. Your energy is no longer wasted in anxiety over what is yours and what is theirs; nor do you concern yourself with winning a favorable opinion from others. When you meditate, you are content with your own self-knowledge. Meditation is self-revealing because it takes you beyond the conditioning of your mind. Other people do not see you with such clarity. They perceive from their own stage of life. Their understanding is colored by their own particular background.

Why, then, accept their definition of you when you know that it is clouded by their own mental conditioning?

If you met a blind person out walking on a lovely, sunny day and asked him what the day looked like, he might answer, "Dark as night." Would you accept his opinion as the truth or would you object and respond with anger saying, "How can you see darkness? It is daytime and the sun is shining!" You would most likely do neither because you would understand that it is bright and sunny for you, but dark for him. You would be aware of his condition. You would neither fight with him, nor take what he says to heart. You would simply accept him as he is, knowing that his perception is limited by his blindness.

Similarly, if someone criticizes you, that is fine. If someone praises you, that, too, is fine. You allow the one to criticize and the other to praise because that is the nature of each; but you rely on neither. Instead, you maintain your equanimity while looking into your own heart for the truth.

There is a beautiful anecdote which exemplifies this sense of inner balance. Once there was a saint meditating under a tree in wintertime. As he was sitting peacefully with his eyes closed, a man who was passing by wearing a beautiful shawl caught sight of him. Thinking the old saint must be feeling the cold, the traveler offered him his shawl. The saint opened his eyes and blessed this generous man saying, "You will do it again and again." The traveler went on his way.

After half an hour, a thief happened by and saw the shawl draped over the shoulders of the saint. He wondered to himself, "Why should a saint be wearing such a costly shawl? I could get a lot of money for a shawl like that." He quickly snatched the shawl away from the saint.

Now the saint again opened his eyes and blessed the thief saying, "Here is my blessing. You will do it again and again." The thief went on his way.

Meanwhile, there was a man sitting in a nearby tree, watching all that went on. He was overcome with curiosity. "What kind of blessings are these?" he asked the saint. "The good man and the thief both received the same words —'You will do it again and again.' Doesn't a saint make any distinction between these two men? Don't you realize that one man gave you a generous gift and the other man stole it away from you?"

The saint answered, "The traveler who gave me the gift has a rich heart. Until the last day of his life, he will give over and over again. Inwardly, he is a wealthy man. The thief, in his turn, will steal again and again. He will know poverty until the last day of his life."

"What does it all mean?" asked the man.

The saint replied, "People's actions are dictated by the way they perceive themselves and the world. Men like the thief have lived in the same conditioned thinking—the same rut—until their inner sense of lack has become a part of their nature. They do not give up this acquired nature easily, but cling to it until the last day. Only *pragnā*, the light of inner wisdom, can transform them; so it is pointless to criticize or be upset by them."

When you understand and accept mankind as the saint in the story did, the pure flow of love from your heart will touch the hearts of all you meet. Your energy will no longer be consumed in criticism or in the pursuit of approval; for you know that the opinions of others are, at best, partial truth. Instead, you will use meditation to penetrate your own reality.

As you meditate, watch your day's activities. Observe exactly how you live—how you act and react. See the nature of your relationship with those around you. Step back and take a look at yourself. If you need some further aid, then seek out a particular guide, a teacher, or a friend who understands you well—someone who sees you clearly and is capable of giving you good insight and unprejudiced advice. Eventually, through persistent observation and meditation, you will gain a new level of understanding and will be able to extend that understanding to the world around you. Wherever you go, you will exude warmth and love.

Now, once we have thoroughly experienced the inner wisdom of the sixth center, through which we observe the world and our lives from a fresh viewpoint, we come at last to the seventh center. This is the highest level of consciousness, the crown center. Here we arrive at the pure consciousness of Self. This state of being is experienced when all resistance, all heaviness, has dropped away. Meditating on the previous six centers, we have gradually been transcending the gravitational forces that pulled us downward. These are the forces of our fluctuating desires, of our negative thinking and emotion. They have kept us in the arena of loss and gain and have imprisoned us in a state of imbalance. With awareness of the seventh center, we win without even the desire to win. Free and light, we naturally attain our highest goal; we come to our Real Nature.

From this point on, we live each moment according to our "suchness," our true essence, remembering that our whole future is contained in the present moment. How we live right now has repercussions even on the day of our departure. Living from the realm of the real and the permanent Self, we have no need to worry about the outcome of our future. All insecurity and inner conflict are dissolved in the light of pure consciousness of Self.

Many students of yoga attempt to raise their *kundalini*, their inner energy, to this center at the top of the head by force through various heavy-breathing techniques. What they do not realize is that the *kundalini* will not remain at this peak unless they have worked on their inner world as we are doing. A violent surge of energy to the top of the head is very dangerous. It would be like a cardiac patient winning the lottery and dying of a heart attack in his excitement. What should be a positive experience can be overwhelming to someone unprepared for it. We should, therefore, move gradually, refining our energy and mastering first one center and then another until we reach the highest point of awareness.

The Sanskrit name for the seventh center is *sahasrāra*, which means "a thousand petals." Symbolically, there are a thousand rays emanating from the center of the *chakra*, like a thousand spokes radiating from the hub of a wheel. We can think of it as the petals of a lotus opening to receive the light of the sun.

Meditating on this center, you will experience all your

duality merging into oneness with the universal life-force. Even at the sixth point of meditation and awareness, we still see separation between I and Thou. At the highest level, however, there is no otherness, there is no separation, no subject and object. There is only oneness.

We are familiar with the Biblical expression "Be still and know that I am God." These are not the words of ego, but of the experience of the seventh center. In the stillness, all the waves and ripples of life's surface subside until nothing remains but "I am." Those who reach this awareness become vessels bearing the divine energy to their fellow beings. They are truly initiated into a new way of life.

Are you aware of how helpful you can be to a divided world once you have fully received the divine energy which is released by your realization of your oneness with the life-force? Your help will come from true knowledge, from your inner light. It will come from the experience of "Be still and know that I am God."

Mankind thirsts for this kind of awareness. Now at the seventh center, you are initiated—by your teacher, by this energy, by your vision, or by your commitment—into a life of sharing this divine energy with those who are in need. Now is the best opportunity to fulfill this mission. You have everything you need: a beautiful body and brain and five senses all intact. All these fine attributes help you receive and share this energy. Just as a millionaire may share his wealth, so you now share yours. Yours is the wealth of your inner life, the wealth of your thinking, and the wealth of your body which is given in service. When you serve mankind out of love from the fullness of your awareness, you never tire. Only when you work for a selfish purpose do you exhaust your resources. Serving through love, your vitality is always replenished.

To meditate on the seventh center, visualize the thousand rays as the petals of a beautiful white lotus turning upward to welcome the sun. Similarly, you are opening yourself at the crown of the head to receive the pure energy of the *siddhas*, all those souls who have reached perfection.

See yourself bathed in bright, white light. All the colors representing all the different costumes of life, the different manifestations of our energy, are ended at this level. There is only pure white light.

Now, silently repeat the mantra *om arhum namah*. *Arhum* means "I am the worthiest energy, pure energy; I am nothing but absolute energy." With this mantra you are saying, "I bow to that absolute energy which I am."

You no longer see separation; no longer will you divide into "I" and "Thou." From the moment you experience this oneness, you are initiated into a new life. Inwardly, you are convinced that your life has a mission: to receive and to share the divine energy.

In reality, we are that absolute energy. We are truly the "That" of *sohum*. We are Love, the Worthiest Energy. *Arhum* is the climax, the culmination, of *sohum*. God is Love expanded, and we are this Love, this expanded Love. As we continue working on these seven centers, we may glimpse for a fraction of a moment in our stillness, the pure consciousness of Self, the Oneness, the egoless experience of "I am God." This powerful experience will illumine all the days of our lives.

CHAPTER VIII

Using the Energy Centers
for Health and Healing

We are like the shining sun, and our sicknesses, like passing clouds which appear to extinguish the sun's rays. The wise person who gazes at the dull, gray sky knows that, in reality, the sun still shines brightly behind the veil of clouds. All that is needed to uncover its radiance is a strong wind.

As we begin to experience our true essence, we will realize that we are not our sicknesses. Our original nature is wholeness—health. We are perfect, infinite energy. We are Ātmā.

Then where do our illnesses come from? All illness of mind, body, or emotions is an effect of our ignorance of this perfect Self. When we are unaware of our intrinsic wholeness, we unwittingly invite our diseases by treating our body carelessly and by burdening our mind and nervous system with negative thoughts and emotions. Through ignorance, we allow ourselves to live in the realm of the limiting ego with its fluctuating anger, greed, and deceit.

We abuse our body with too much of the wrong kinds of food and too little rest and exercise.

As we become aware of our perfect nature, we can begin to participate consciously in the healing process. We can use meditation to discover the fundamental causes of any disease and begin to reestablish inner physical and emotional harmony.

The first secret of healing is acceptance of health. Before you can begin to enjoy abundant health, you must possess the unshakable conviction that nature's tendency is to heal, to regain and maintain the natural balance. This means that you must stop anticipating illness—expecting sickness to overtake you tomorrow, next winter, in old age, or whenever. The anxiety itself creates the environment for disease. It sets in motion a vicious circle in which inner negative expectations affect the outer circumstances which, in turn, trigger negative responses in your physical and mental system. You must begin to take notice of the interaction among mind, emotions, and the physical organism. How we feel about ourselves affects the way we conduct our lives and ultimately influences our health.

What we believe inwardly is eventually reflected outwardly; so as we build health in our consciousness, we will one day see health mirrored in the physical body. We receive—health, energy, and a sense of well-being—according to the extent of our belief.

Now, as you begin to accept the possibility of your inborn wholeness, observe the unique nature of your individual metabolism. No two bodies are exactly alike. Watch. How do the seasons affect your energy? How does the food you eat affect your digestion? What is the right amount of food for you? Remember that the food you eat today becomes the cells of your body tomorrow. Be aware of the materials with which you choose to build this body. Take the time to be your own observer and be open to the clues your body gives you about its condition and its needs.

As you begin to accept responsibility for the state of your health, you are ready to link the energy centers to the healing and health-maintaining process. When you meditate on the first center, you are focusing your attention and health-giving energy on the earth element, which corresponds to the bone, skin, nails, and hair of your body. Remember that this center is located at the base of the spine, which is a vital part of your skeletal structure.

In mastering this first center, you are psychologically freeing yourself from the need to seek security in accumulating external things. This includes the desire to take in food beyond the body's capacity to digest it. It includes also the unchecked craving for those foods which are nonnourishing or even harmful.

Meditating on this center reestablishes our conscious contact with the body. We become sensitive to the nutritional demands of our particular metabolism. Our tendency to overeat diminishes, and we begin to cultivate a new taste for healthy, life-giving foods.

When you bring your attention to the second center, you are tuning in to the vital energy of the water element, which is present in all the bodily fluids. Through the circulation of the blood, the water element is present in the body's entire system of supplying nutrients and removing waste from each and every cell. It is also key to your digestion. The digestive process begins, in fact, the moment your food comes in contact with your saliva.

To appreciate the importance of this essential element, it may be helpful to keep in mind that the body is composed of 90 percent water. When functioning properly, our bodily fluids are an integral part of our body's life-support system. What happens, however, when we introduce the negative element of tension? We are all familiar with the adverse effects of emotional strain. It can increase our pulse rate, raise our blood pressure, and eventually lead to heart disease. In addition, the chemical balance in saliva can be severely altered by stress. The result will affect our digestion and can damage our teeth.

So, when we meditate on the second center, we watch for the source of stress which upsets the equilibrium of the water element within the body. We pay attention, for example, to the subtle forms of deceit which cloud our natural spontaneity and ensnare us in a ceaseless game of projections and second-guessing. We are the ultimate victims of our deceit, for it takes a great deal of our energy to uphold the smallest lie and to maintain a false impression. Even our dreams reflect our unspoken anxiety, so we watch these also.

Meditation on the second center will make you more keenly aware of those inner tensions which impede the natural flow of your bodily fluids. Seeking the source of your stress, you can root it out and begin to enjoy the fruits of a new serenity.

The third center, at the navel, is a direct link with the

stomach and intestinal area. The fire element is that physical energy which generates bodily heat and aids the digestion. Psychologically, you may experience the imbalance of the fire element in the emotion of anger. This sets off a chain of negative reactions throughout the body that may show up as indigestion. It is, therefore, advisable not to eat when angry. Take care that you dine when you are in a pleasant, relaxed mood. In that way, your emotions will aid the healthy functioning of the entire body.

Watch your anger. It can be triggered by the most trivial things. It may be very subtle. When we attempt to get people to act as we desire them to or try to manipulate events to conform to our plan, we lay ourselves open to anger. In our rage, whether expressed or not, we upset our whole metabolism.

The fourth center, located in the area of the heart, brings you in touch with the gift of breath—the air element. We must begin to appreciate this precious element. Each breath is the means for the exchange of carbon dioxide for oxygen at the cell level. Oxygen is absolutely necessary to the activity of the brain. We cannot survive without it. Even our pores breathe!

Proper breathing is essential to our vitality. Have you ever noticed someone who is angry and upset? His breathing is quick and shallow. How many of us allow tension, fear, anxiety, and simple laziness to shorten each breath and undermine the body's health? The practice of *prāna yāma* breathing is a great energizer and a good way to get us in the habit of breathing deeply. Each deep breath helps to calm the nervous system and bring about a new level of inner tranquility.

[80]

As you focus on this heart center, you will also see that the tendency toward high blood pressure and heart attacks is exacerbated by a life driven by the ego. This ego is anxiety-producing. It demands that we write our name on the flowing water of time. How long can we fool ourselves? Deep inside we know that, in reality, time will dissolve the ego and our name will one day be forgotten. So what are we trying to prove, and to whom? Other people are absorbed in their own worry. They are immersed in the dissolving of their own egos as they move along with the stream of time.

When you recognize that this limited "me" is but a small point in eternity, you can put an end to the inner battle to prove and to grab at worldly recognition. Let go of that ego which spoils your relationships and fosters inner tension. Meditating on *sohum*, dissolve this brittle ego and discover the Real Self. Allow the vast river of love to flow between you and others, and moment by moment, begin to make the experience of life itself eternal.

You can psychologically begin to relieve much of the congestion in the area of the ears, nose, and throat as you meditate on the fifth energy center. This is the center for vocal expression, inner purity, and space. We all have a need for sufficient physical, mental, and emotional space. Unfortunately, we tend to forget that unexpressed emotion and unresolved conflicts clog our inner space. Held inside, they eventually erupt like a volcano and appear on the physical plane, begging for our attention. They show up in the form of headaches or rashes, and any number of other uncomfortable symptoms. Suppression is obviously no solution to our problems.

With meditation, you can learn to express your feelings gently and genuinely, creating a new sense of harmony and inner spaciousness. Relieved of the pressure of accumulated frustrations, the mind can relax and the emotions can flow naturally. Free of their silent burden, the mind, body, and emotions will begin to cooperate with one another to form a healthy, integrated whole.

The first five centers are direct links to our physical organism. Meditation on these centers helps us to maintain the proper balance of basic elements in our makeup.

The sixth center is the point from which our heightened awareness can observe the workings of the first five. From this point you can note what the nature of your illness is and at which center your energy appears to be blocked. Watching your body, mind, and emotions and being aware of your food, energy, and physical activity, you know where correction is needed. With proper knowledge of your own individual condition, you are able to take those measures which will ensure the maintenance of maximum health. Prevention is better than cure, for it takes a great deal of energy to bring about a cure. Therefore, we cannot afford to neglect our health today. Sooner or later, we will pay for our negligence.

The seventh center transcends the bounds of our physical organism. When you are truly one with your whole, permanent, inner Self, there is no room for sickness. At this highest point of awareness, you no longer identify with the passing clouds of illness. You know without doubt that you are perfect, absolute, conscious energy. You are the shining sun.

CHAPTER IX

An Integrated Meditation
on the Seven Energy Centers

The ancient seers spent their lives searching for the inner workings of man. Their laboratory was man's inner world. Their investigation depended on inner perception, concentration, and self-observation. They strove to be impartial observers of the processes of action, reaction, and interaction.

In order to be free of all outer distractions, they chose quiet mountaintops and caves for their places of meditation. They knew that one must be in balance if one wished to be able to see clearly the subtle interplay of man's thoughts, emotions, dreams, and physical sensations.

They searched for the hidden cause behind their outer circumstances. Gradually, they understood that the atmosphere people created around themselves was directly related to the level of their own consciousness. For example, the kind of people we attract is determined by the invisible atmosphere we have constructed by our state of awareness at a given time. If we evolve away from that level to a new

[83]

level of awareness, we will eventually witness a subsequent transformation in our outer circumstances and circle of friends.

In the course of their research, these wise people discovered a new spiritual world unknown to many people. This is the world of the Higher Self, the level of Pure Awareness. They knew that every individual possessed a Higher Self and could, with practice, reach this pure level of awareness. They knew also that they could communicate with their fellowman from this pure Self rather than from the uncertain level of changing desires and petty jealousies. They understood that the meaning and purpose of man's life lay in the continuing evolution of his consciousness.

Therefore, all our activities, all our practices are simply the means for our evolution. If we keep this idea in mind, all that we do in life will be connected to this purpose. Our activities will no longer be random and fragmented.

Now, the question is, how do we evolve? What is evolution? Evolution is expansion. Whenever we expand, we are evolving. Our human form has evolved from a single cell into a multiplicity of cells. We have enlarged our structure. Now we must expand our consciousness and, in the process, maintain inner balance and harmony. We must free ourselves of all antagonistic feelings, all feelings of alienation. We can then begin to experience the tranquility and lightness of heart which springs from our oneness with the universe.

We have been exploring a series of meditations in which we learn to focus on each energy center individually. In this way, we become familiar with our innate vitality. We know its several aspects, its best uses, and we learn to channel our energy appropriately.

We now go one step further and incorporate all seven centers in one meditation. Originally, this meditation was practiced out-of-doors on a mountaintop, or on a seashore, or any place from which the meditator could have an unobstructed view of the natural horizon. So, if you have the opportunity to be in the mountains or by the sea, you can follow the example of the ancient seers by meditating outdoors. If you are in the city or indoors, you may use your imagination to visualize a natural environment where there is a clear horizon.

The first step is to sit in the fresh air, someplace where the air is able to move freely. Secondly, begin by practicing *prāna yāma* breathing: inhale, retain the breath, exhale. (For a description of *prāna yāma* breathing, see the fifth chapter.) This exercise can be repeated twelve times. The third step in this procedure is to follow this breathing exercise with the mantra *hrim*.* The sound of *hrim*, your own inner power, evokes the universal energy. The universe responds to your vibration.

The fourth step is to allow your gaze to rest on the ground right in front of you. Your eyes are half-closed. There is no force or tension; you are simply sitting in a relaxed mood and resting your gaze on the ground directly before you. Now, the fifth step: Slowly lift your gaze to a middle point somewhere between where you are seated and the horizon. You may fix your eyes on some object or simply on a line of direction. Rest at this point of focus

---

* For a full explanation of the use of *hrim*, see Chitrabhanu, *Realize What You Are: The Fundamentals of Jain Meditation.*

for 30 to 40 seconds. Then, the sixth step is to raise your gaze gradually to the horizon itself. In effect, you are stretching your vision to the limit, to the horizon line.

The seventh step is to bring your gaze slowly back, first to the middle point, then to the ground directly before you; and finally, to close the eyes. The eighth step is to repeat this entire visual exercise in your imagination with your inner awareness. You have, in effect, absorbed your outer environment. You have brought your outer world into your inner world. This whole procedure takes seven to eight minutes. There is no haste, no time pressure.

Now, the vision which has been stretched to encompass the outer horizon is turned inward toward each center. Bring your inner attention to the first center. Feel and experience the center as you rest your inner gaze there. Then use the mantra for this center. Except for *sohum*, which is generally repeated silently along with the breath, these mantras may be either articulated or voiced inwardly. When you feel you have touched upon the essence of this center, move slowly to the next center. You are now climbing gradually upward through all seven centers.

Keep in mind that in this procedure, you look out before you look in. First observe your outward surroundings so that the desire to see the outside world will not remain in your mind and disturb your concentration. Then, look in before looking up. You turn your attention inward by beginning to focus on the centers which manifest your inner energy. Observe whether or not your energy is being used creatively and positively. Finally, look up. Looking up refers to your gradual movement upward toward finer and finer levels of awareness until you reach the highest level, consciousness of Self. As long as your gaze or your attention is downward, you will not be able to perceive this Higher Self, this divinity within.

As you move through the various stages of consciousness, you will first experience a new steadiness. You will no longer fluctuate between happiness and depression, between "can I" or "can't I," between "shall I" or "shan't I." You will feel sure and steady.

Next, you will be able to withdraw from the attraction of sensual desires. This does not mean you withdraw from the world; but you will be able to determine when and how to use your senses and when to pull back. You will be like the turtle, which knows how to withdraw in the face of a threat in order to protect itself. You will no longer be the slave of physical desires.

Gradually, you will enjoy a new inner tranquility. Imagine the icy surface of a lake in winter. It has no ripples. No sudden wind can disturb its calm surface. One can skate across the lake, free of the thought of drowning. Similarly, your equanimity will not be upset by the wind and waves of changing moods and circumstances.

Now you come to the state of inner radiation. At this point of awareness, your inner world is now as vivid to you as the outer world has previously appeared to be.

Finally, you reach the height of consciousness which is beyond all the previous levels of consciousness. This is the supreme moment of consummation with one's Self.

How do you incorporate this meditation on all seven centers into your daily meditation routine? If you are in the country for the weekend or on vacation, simply begin with your regular morning meditation and follow it with the procedure I have just given you.

However, during your normal workweek, it is better to practice your morning meditation as usual and reserve some time each evening to focus on just one of the centers. Concentrate on one center for a whole week and then move on to the next one the following week. After seven weeks, begin again with the first center. This way, there would be no time pressure on you. You would be relaxed and at ease.

As you gradually begin to experience these centers fully, you will be able to connect readily with the element or essence of each center: earth, water, fire, air, space, mind, and consciousness of Self. Being in tune with each aspect of your innate energy, you will be able to heal body and mind and maintain inner balance.

To understand, to experience, and to master each center takes patience and practice. It may take years. One day, you will be Master of your body, Master of your mind, and Master of your Self. The whole idea behind this meditation is to become this Master.

APPENDIX

Summary Chart of the Seven Energy Centers

Appendix

chakra:	Mulādhāra	Swādhisthāna	Manipura
meaning:	root/support	your own dwelling/origin	jewel city
quality:	security	creativity	expansiveness/power/expression
area:	base of spine	pelvis	navel
symbol:	square/cross	crescent moon	triangle
color:	yellow	silver	red/yellow
mantra:	shivam shānti	mano ramam	rām
meaning:	benediction & peace	mind-player	the indweller who gives life to the mind, body and senses
element:	earth	water	fire
sense:	smell	taste	sight

Appendix

SEVEN ENERGY CENTERS

Anāhata	Vishuddha	Ājnā	Sahasrāra
that which is ever-new	pure amidst all purity/holy amongst the holiest	command	thousand petals
love	abundance/ space/purity/ power of speech	clarity/ insight/ inner command	higher consciousness
heart	throat	center of brow	crown of the head
circle	oval	third eye	thousand petals/ thousand rays
sky-blue	mauve	orange/ whole spectrum of color	white
sohum	aim	pragnā	om arhum namah
I am That	energy of wisdom, purity, plenty	wisdom (with compassion)	I bow to the worthiest energy which I am
air	space	mind/thought	consciousness of Self
touch	hearing